Pedals,]
Cobblestones

Ritchie Greenwood

Copyright © 2018 Ritchie Greenwood

ISBN: 978-0-244-97463-3

All rights reserved, including the right to reproduce this book, or portions thereof in any form. No part of this text may be reproduced, transmitted, downloaded, decompiled, reverse engineered, or stored, in any form or introduced into any information storage and retrieval system, in any form or by any means, whether electronic or mechanical without the express written permission of the author.

Every effort has been made to obtain the necessary permissions with reference to copyright material. We apologise for any omissions in this respect and will be pleased to make the appropriate acknowledgements in any future edition.

PublishNation
www.publishnation.co.uk

This work is dedicated to all the Jacks, Olives and Spencers that have suffered maltreatment, abuse and murder at the hands of mankind and that have never been fortunate enough to experience the unconditional love they themselves give so freely.

Ritchie lives with his wife Chriss and their two Spanish rescue dogs, Olive and Spencer on the Fylde Coast in Lancashire. He still rides his bike several times a week and both of them are still involved with supporting and fundraising for animal rescues.

He hasn't written anything since.

Contents

The Starfish Story	2
Palmares	3
Glossary	4
Foreword	5
Prologue	6
The Chosen One	8
Life's Too Short to Ride Shit Bikes	14
These Aren't the Droids You're Looking For	21
Baptism of Fire	26
I Predict a Riot	37
The Hell of the North	44
Dawgs, Dya Like Dawgs	51
Adopt Don't Shop	59
A Saturday in Hell	69
A Seed is Sown	96
Three is the Magic Number	101
Ride for Rescue	110
Race Day Remembrance	120
Never Say Never Again	125
Straight Outta Compton	136
It Ain't Half Hot Mum	142
Donation Donation Donation	154
Epilogue	161
Afterword	166
Acknowledgements	167

The Starfish Story

Once upon a time, there was an old man who used to go to the ocean to do his writing. He had a habit of walking on the beach every morning before he began his work. Early one morning, he was walking along the shore after a big storm had passed and found the vast beach littered with starfish as far as the eye could see, stretching in both directions.

Off in the distance, the old man noticed a small boy approaching. As the boy walked, he paused every so often and as he grew closer, the man could see that he was occasionally bending down to pick up an object and throw it into the sea. The boy came closer still and the man called out, "Good morning! May I ask what it is that you are doing?"

The young boy paused, looked up, and replied "Throwing starfish into the ocean. The tide has washed them up onto the beach and they can't return to the sea by themselves," the youth replied. "When the sun gets high, they will die, unless I throw them back into the water."

The old man replied, "But there must be tens of thousands of starfish on this beach. I'm afraid you won't really be able to make much of a difference."

The boy bent down, picked up yet another starfish and threw it as far as he could into the ocean. Then he turned, smiled and said, "It made a difference to that one!"

adapted from The Star Thrower, by Loren Eiseley

Palmares

Nov '94	Sydney to the Gong	110km
July '02	Manchester Blackpool	100km
May '09	Welsh 3000s (Hike)	
Aug '14	Manchester100	161km
April '15	Paris Roubaix Challenge	171km
May '15	Cheshire Cobbled Classic	100km
Aug '15	Manchester100	161km
Oct '15	Liverpool Roubaix	100km
April '16	Ronde Van Vlaanderen Cyclo	135km
April '16	Paris Roubaix Challenge	171km
May '16	Roman Road Challenge	146km
July '16	White Roads Classic (DNF)	
July '16	L'Etape du Tour	125km
Sept '16	Liverpool Roubaix	100km
April '17	Liege-Bastogne-Liege Challenge	157km

Glossary

Berg	Hill
Bidon	Water bottle
Broom Wagon	Last vehicle collecting riders unable to finish the race in time permitted
Col	Mountain
Century	One hundred mile bike ride
Chapeau	Hats off/ well done
Classics	Prestigious one day professional bike races
DNF	Did Not Finish
Drops	Bottom part of the handlebars
Etape	Stage
Flanders	Region of Belgium
Galgo Espanol	Spanish greyhound
MAMIL	Middle Aged Man In Lycra
Monument	Most iconic & prestigious one day race in the professional cycling calendar
Musette	Small cotton shoulder bag used in cycling to carry food
Muur	Dutch for wall
Peloton	Group of riders
Palmares	Accomplishments
Pave	Cobblestone
Podenco	Hound
Ronde	Tour
Secteur	Section of road
Soigneur	Assistant (French for 'one who provides care')
Sportive	Organised amateur cycling event
Train	Fast moving single/double line of riders
UCI	Union Cycliste Internationale- World governing body for sport of cycling
Velodrome	Arena for track cycling
Vlaanderen	Dutch for Flanders

Foreword

April 2017
Liege, Belgium

I'm standing at the window of our hotel room peering out through the drawn drapes into the gloom of a typically grey and miserable Belgian spring morning. As I watch the raindrops fall onto the adjacent roofs listening to Alan, still soundly asleep judging by the noise of his breathing, my mind wanders back to events which happened just over two years ago.

The inclement weather is also reminiscent of that day which not only was the catalyst for my Challenge but the writing of this book and the fundamental story contained herein.

Suddenly jerking me from my nostalgic trip down memory lane Alans alarm starts to sound.

Today we have a date with 'The Old Lady' but what we don't yet realise is how cruel and unrelentingly harsh she can be. It's a menage a trois the like of which neither of us will ever forget nor ever wish to repeat I think it fair to say.

Alan may one day share his painful memories of that day with his grandchildren whereas I being childless will take them unspoken into the afterlife whatever that may be.

The others I'm going to share with *you*.

Prologue

'When man invented the bicycle he reached the peak of his attainments.'
Elizabeth West (author)

'They' whoever 'they' are say that everyone has a book in them. 'They' also say that you should write about a subject you know something about.

I've considered writing a book about cycling for some time now but never started as I thought who would want to read *my* book of cycling exploits, but having said that I've read plenty of books about cycling by ordinary people which led me to think 'well why the hell not'. What I didn't want to happen was for it to become some kind of travel guide and training manual, all athletes get to know their own bodies so well that they find what works for them and what works for me probably won't work for you. Nor did I want it to become a cathartic exorcism of the demons from my childhood.

Anyway here's my one book which is about cycling, dogs and charity fundraising. There won't be a sequel or even a prequel, this is as 'they' say *it*.

I know an awful lot about cycling, a little bit about dogs but the only knowledge I have of fundraising is what I learnt during the course of the first half of 2016.

I spent quite a while deliberating over the title of this book as to begin with I'd convinced myself it should be cycling related. However a fellow dog walker had called me a 'dog whisperer' which at first seemed like an appropriate title but makes no reference to the actual catalysts for writing the book. Therefore I finally decided upon a title which I felt reflected the intrinsic elements of the story.

You could call this my memoir, even though the main part of the story only covers a short period of my life it undoubtedly covers the most important and rewarding period thus far.

I don't believe in God or religion. I understand some people feel the need to put their faith in something but in a modern world of scientific knowledge and rational I find it totally irrational to say a flash flood was an act of God or a seven year old child dying of leukaemia was Gods will.

I do however believe in fate, that certain things happen for a reason and that most of the time things have a habit of working out for the better. As you will read throughout the course of this book there have been several occasions where there is no doubt in my mind that fate has played a defining part in my life.

I also believe that sometimes something chooses you and you have no conscious control over that. I believe that to be the case in me having from a very early age a passion for anything involving two wheels.

Ultimately that passion has led me on this journey to where I am today relating to you my story of cycling, dogs and charity fundraising.

Enjoy the ride.

The Chosen One

'As a kid I had a dream, I wanted to own my own bicycle. When I got the bike I must have been the happiest boy in Liverpool, maybe the world. I lived for that bike.'
John Lennon (founding member of The Beatles)

Cycling chose me. I didn't choose it. I'm convinced of that.

I've been cycling for well over thirty years now but let me start at the beginning.

I grew up in a small village called Edenfield nestled in the Rossendale valley in east Lancashire approximately fifteen miles north of Manchester. When I was a young boy in the late seventies Edenfield was affectionately known by the local populace as 'the magic village'. This wasn't in a benevolent Harry Potter kind of way but because it had developed a reputation for hard drinking, drug taking, partying and fighting. At the epicentre of this culture was my father. Everybody knew who the Greenwoods were, my mum worked every pub bar in the village as a second job at some point, and everyone knew of my father and his fearsome reputation. He was a hard man my dad but not in a good way. He had a real mean nasty argumentative streak which had a habit of surfacing following one of his many drinking binges.

I've heard all the legendary stories of his exploits of drinking, womanising and fighting from his best friend, another of the major players from those halcyon days. The police were always knocking on our door wanting to feel his collar for something or other and he was always coming home having lost his job because he'd had a 'do' with someone he couldn't get along with hence, my mother usually having a second job to keep the family afloat. God knows how or why she put up with him, she loved him I guess. I also know that he had a pretty shitty upbringing but for me part of the responsibility of being a parent is to give your child a better start in life than you had.

From a very early age I promised myself I wouldn't be like him as well as pledging never to have children of my own, after all I didn't want to take the risk of becoming the kind of father he had been. As the saying goes the apple doesn't fall far from the tree.

Needless to say we didn't have a very good relationship which only deteriorated as I became older and began to question his behaviour which led to me bearing the brunt of his vicious temper on many occasions. I learnt to run really fast really quick. I never saw him laugh, not a proper laugh anyway, at best you'd get a strained smile. On reflection I think he was a deeply unhappy person who didn't get much pleasure from life and was quite disgruntled at the way his life had turned out even though much of it had been of his own making. A troubled soul of that there's no doubt.

What does he think? It doesn't matter what he thinks, he's dead. He's been dead a long time.

He died of bladder cancer the day before my eighteenth birthday so I subsequently spent my coming of age organising a funeral, the irony of which I'm sure wouldn't have been lost on him, so he's been dead a lot longer than he was actually a part of my life.

My mother is the youngest of four girls who were tragically left motherless when my maternal grandmother died on my mum's seventh birthday (my paternal grandfather also coincidentally died on my mum's birthday many years later, both from lung cancer) so her childhood wasn't that great either. Maybe things might have turned out totally differently had her mum survived. As it was she and her sisters had to fend for themselves whilst my grandfather worked every hour god sent trying to provide for his family. I think she's carried a chip on her shoulder about this her whole life. She's a Gemini which probably explains the mood swings and fiery temper. Her idea of parenting was 'children should be seen and not heard' and she wasn't afraid to use physical violence to instil discipline. My relationship with her is what I suppose could best be described as difficult. She and my sister have always been very close but we never have and I've always felt like an outsider, the black sheep of the family. The last conversation I had with her some considerable time ago involved how she had parented us whereupon I told her that her actions nowadays would at best have seen us placed in care, at worst she'd have been locked up. Her response was to laugh at me.

My sister and I rarely see each other or even speak to each other from one year to the next. She left home at eighteen and went to university in Liverpool to study law having known from the age of twelve she wanted to be a barrister. At that age I didn't even know what the fuck a barrister was, I was too busy recreating the battle for Goose Green with my toy soldiers. She's a very clever girl our kid and could have been anything she wanted, brain surgeon, rocket scientist you name it she has got the intelligence, dedication and focus to be it. She's lived overseas for several years having married an American diplomat so we don't even have our annual Christmas visit anymore. We have very different ideas about justice and the legal system which often leads to heated debate, she believes everyone deserves a chance to be rehabilitated whereas I think once you cross that line you give up the rights afforded to decent law abiding citizens. 'An eye for an eye, a tooth for a tooth' is my philosophy. Something we do have in common though is that we're both stress heads and short tempered. Genetic defects inherited from our parents I'm afraid.

I have ten cousins, three aunties and two uncles still alive as far as I know, none of whom I'd recognise if I walked past them in the street. The only other surviving relative I have that I visit a couple of times a year is my father's auntie Evelyn who is a dead ringer for Ronnie Corbett.

Whoever said you can choose your friends but you can't choose your family must have had us in mind when he coined the phrase. And, all that bullshit about blood being thicker than water is exactly that, bullshit.

The very first recollection I have of any sensory stimulation relating to anything involving two wheels was when I was a small child of maybe four or five years old. A work colleague of my fathers had stopped by our house to show off his new motorcycle. I remember how big and loud the bike was, he was dressed head to toe in black leather reeking of Brut33, he certainly had splashed it all over. If my young mind could have understood the emotions I was feeling I'd have described them as almost akin to a state of sexual arousal.

I suppose it's ironic that one of the few gifts my father gave me is the one gift that has kept giving all my life and provided me with the most pleasure and satisfaction. That gift was teaching me how to ride a bicycle. Back then there were no fancy balance bikes, I don't think stabilizers were even available, I certainly never used them. As with virtually every other kid from my generation I was taught using the traditionally old fashioned method of being held upright, urged by the adult to trust them and take your feet off the ground, them running behind holding the saddle whilst you gingerly turned the pedals gaining momentum then promptly falling off when you glanced over your shoulder only to see they'd let go. Sobbing, feeling sorry for yourself and your skinned knee being told not to be so soft and give it another go, wiping your snotty nose on your sleeve and building up the courage to go again. Then the unforgettable feeling of joy and euphoria at discovering your balance point and riding off down the street a huge smile enveloping your face.

My mother was never taught to ride a bicycle which seems so completely alien to me, I imagine there are more people unable to read or write than unable ride a bicycle. She is quick to point out that she can roller skate but who cares about roller skating when you can go cycling. I don't think it can be overestimated how important a bicycle is in a child's life, that first sense of freedom and adventure it provides them with and the simple pleasure it brings. My mother has never known that, little wonder then she seems such an unhappy person.

In recent years cycling has become very popular but when I were a lad most people never touched a bicycle once they were past adolescence unlike in mainland Europe where cycling is very much ingrained in the culture. However a chance encounter during the school summer holidays of 1986, would change my life forever ensuring I became one of the few, not the many.

I remember it being a balmy midsummers evening sometime in July, I was playing out with Paddy who lived a few doors down the street, which kids of my generation did back then as there were no Xbox's or internet, when a lad from my school year sped past in a blur on a green racing bicycle. Justin wasn't a friend of mine, well not then he wasn't, but we were acquainted as we had a couple of classes together. I called out to him as he went flying up the road not expecting him to hear me but he looked over his shoulder, slowed, performed a U-turn then rolled to a stop outside my house. I was mistaken his bicycle wasn't green it was turquoise, the colour is actually 'celeste blue', with the word **BIANCHI** (pronounced by-an-key) stamped on the sloping down tube in bold black letters.

Bianchi is to cycling what Ferrari is to Formula One and celeste blue is equally as iconic as rosso red. Seeing a Ferrari that isn't rosso red seems completely incongruous, which is exactly the same feeling with a Bianchi that isn't celeste blue. Since 1885 the Italian company Bianchi has been producing bicycles and is the oldest bicycle manufacturer still in existence. One of the greatest professionals ever Fausto 'il Campanissimo' (the champions champion) Coppi famously rode their bicycles with much success throughout his illustrious career, since when Bianchi have been a popular choice by teams within the professional peloton.

Justin clad completely in lycra, tells me how he started cycling last autumn and is just on his way home to Rawtenstall after riding down to Bury, a distance of approximately twenty five miles. I'm impressed. However I'm even more impressed when he tells me that he rides on average about a hundred miles a week. He reluctantly succumbs to my requests to let me have a go. Immediately I'm struck by how fast the bike feels, the speed rising dramatically as the slightest amount of pressure is applied to the pedals. The feeling is fantastic.

Reluctantly I return the bike to him not failing to notice the worried look on his face.

He asks me 'Have you been watching the Tour?' A puzzled expression crosses my face 'The Tour, what's that?' He explains what 'the Tour' is. As he nonchalantly throws his leg over the top tube he tells me 'You've missed it tonight anyway, but check it out.' In no time he's disappeared up the road.

The following evening I'm glued to the television waiting for that nights thirty minute highlight programme of the days racing from the Tour de France on Channel 4. Nowadays due to satellite television there are literally hundreds of channels to choose from however back in 1986 you had a choice of only four and Channel 4 was still in its infancy having only been on air since 2nd November 1982. I remember watching the very first programme ever shown, 'Countdown' which I've been a dedicated follower of ever since.

I'm completely mesmerised and immediately hooked by what I witness.

Life's Too Short to Ride Shit Bikes

'Don't buy upgrades, ride up grades.'
Eddy Merckx (GOAT- Greatest Of All Time)

It's more than thirty years since I watched that first Tour highlights show, since then I've probably watched over five hundred other episodes so it's fair to say the years have the dulled the memories somewhat. What I do recall with complete clarity is during that first show a vignette to the music of 'Atomic' by Blondie was shown which convinced me I wanted to be a cyclist. The clip showed skinny, tanned men clad in brightly coloured lycra drenched in sweat gurning up huge mountain passes, the alpine scenery stunning under the blazing summer sun, riders flying down twisting descents at breakneck speeds even the motorcycles struggling to keep up. There are sprints, crashes, riders hurtling off the edges of mountain roads and a stage win being celebrated by two men cycling side by side arms aloft holding hands sharing the greatest of victories.

I learn that the two men winning at Alpe d'Huez, one of the most iconic climbs ridden in the Tour, are Bernard Hinault and Greg Lemond who are at the absolute pinnacle of the sport. Hinault a Frenchman has already joined a very elite club sealing his name in the record books for immortality as a five time Tour winner and has a fearsome reputation within the peloton, his nicknames of 'Le Patron' and 'the Badger' perfectly illustrate this. Badgers are notoriously aggressive when cornered and will fight to the death. Le Patron literally means 'the boss' who traditionally was the strongest most respected rider in the peloton. Such was the authority of Le Patron that it wasn't uncommon for riders to have to ask his permission to even launch an attack or take a comfort break. Hinault was the last true incarnation of this position amongst his peers, Lance Armstrong attempted to adopt the role but I think it fair to say his authority never really extended beyond the Tour de France. Lemond is the American interloper of an extremely European jingoistic sport, wearing the maillot jaune (yellow jersey of race leader) and is on course for what will become the first of three Tour wins.

Both men ride for the superteam La Vie Claire formed by the Swiss millionaire Bernard Tapie which has dominated the sport since its formation in 1984. Despite the pictures at Alpe d'Huez seeming to show a harmonious relationship between the two riders there has actually been a period of acrimony building up since the '85 Tour. Lemond was in a perfect position to win the race the previous year as Hinault capitulated during a bad day in the mountains but was instructed in no uncertain terms by Tapie to play the honourable team mate and forego his own ambitions to help Hinault secure his fifth Tour. In return for this favour it was agreed Hinault would ride for Lemond and assist him in every way possible to win the following year. However Hinault seemed to have his own agenda.

From the get go Hinault in true badger fashion seemed to attack Lemond at every opportunity even to the point of encouraging Lemonds rivals to join him and assist his attacks. Lemond, a very placid laidback character, was not only visibly shaken but also chagrined by Hinaults antics. When questioned about his unfriendly tactics Hinault responded by saying he did it for Lemonds own good to prove he was a worthy winner of the Tour. A Frenchman has not won the Tour since Hinault.

With team mates like that who needs enemies.

Lemond was lauded as the perfect athletic specimen with a massive VO2 threshold and destined for great things. VO2 measures how much oxygen can be efficiently metabolised by the muscular system before the build-up of lactic acid renders the body exhausted. However he was unfortunately involved in a hunting accident later that year when he was mistakenly shot by his brother in law. He came about as close to dying as was possible and was told by doctors he only survived the blood loss due to having the physiology of an elite athlete. He eventually recovered from his injuries returning to racing to win the '89 Tour by the closest margin ever of eight seconds over Frenchman and double Tour winner Laurent 'the Professor' Fignon on the final day after a classic three week battle. Unsurprisingly there has never been a time trial in Paris on the final day of the Tour ever since. He managed to grind out a third victory the following year but was pretty much a spent force thereafter, the lead pellets which were poisoning his body curtailing his career.

Less than two weeks after that chance encounter with Justin I'm sat on the number 473 bus heading to Bury, world famous for its black pudding, clad in full La Vie Claire cycling team kit on my way to pick up my new road bike. My sister Celestine has leant me the princely sum of one hundred pounds (about £250 in today's money) to purchase coincidentally enough a Dawes Celeste. I'll never forget that first ride, it was only a distance of approximately eight miles but I was absolutely fucked after about six. I had a long long way to go, literally.

Justin and I started cycling together regularly and were soon joined by two other lads from his class Ricky and Stuart both of whom rode Dawes machines as well. Before long we had joined the local cycling club Rossendale Road Club becoming regulars on the traditional Sunday club runs and taking part in junior races. We ate, slept and breathed cycling, fuelling our young enthusiastic minds and bodies voracious appetite for all things cycling. If we weren't actually out cycling we were watching, talking or reading about it. I even started skipping classes at school much preferring a bike ride to the dreadful tedium of double physics.

That first bike was truly horrible though. It was made of steel which meant it was heavy, with cheap components and in no time had started making a dull clanking noise from the bottom bracket every time I turned the cranks. It had to go, so I saved every penny I possibly could from pocket money and paper rounds. About six months later I became the proud owner of a Raleigh Triathlon which aside from the insipid vomit colour was a young cyclists dream. It was full of the latest technology, featuring the new Shimano 105 indexed gear system with the gear shifters incorporated into the brake levers and biopace chainrings to increase the efficiency of your pedal stroke, mounted on an aluminium Reynolds 531 racing frameset. Also I removed the traditional yet outdated toe clip and strap pedals in favour of the new *Look* clipless type, based on ski bindings which helped improve the transfer of power especially on climbs as you can push and pull on the pedals. It was stiff, light, fast and handled brilliantly. I loved that bike and to this day regret selling it to help pay for my plane ticket to Australia. I literally begged, borrowed and stole to get that bike as well.

Since then I'm not afraid to admit that I've always been a bit of a bike snob. Riding a quality bike rather than a cheap one is like going from driving a Mini to a Porsche. Some people might argue that there's no point riding a five grand bike if you've got five pound legs, which is true but the dramatic difference will only serve to improve your riding in the long run. Nowadays I ride a stunning orange and black Trek Domane which turns heads and attracts lots of attention everywhere I go. It's fast, light and comfortable incorporating a high quality carbon frame with a full Shimano Ultegra groupset and aerodynamic Mavic Cosmic wheels giving a fabulously smooth ride.

It seems that nowadays we live in a throwaway society where if something breaks rather than have it fixed we simply purchase a new one. Encouraging this ethos is how readily available cheap finance is, whereas when I was lad finance was very difficult to arrange not to mention extortionately expensive. The philosophy of my childhood tended to be *neither a lender nor a borrower be.* I remember we waited months to save up the money to buy a new television which seems ridiculous to think now that it was such a big deal it turned into a family day out when we eventually purchased it. If you so desire today it's possible to buy a top end Pinarello as ridden by Chris Froome on zero percent finance and pay it back on the never never.

What happens to the majority of teenage boys at some point is that they become aware of the fairer sex and develop an interest in other hedonistic distractions such as alcohol, drugs and partying. Many an aspiring athlete has been lost to these forbidden fruits. At the time I was completely immersed in cycling, so much so that one day I happened to overhear my father asking my mother if I might be gay wearing all that colourful lycra and shaving my legs. I had to stifle a laugh but that was exactly the sort of reaction I'd come to expect from him. Rather than become interested in my hobby he preferred the company of his pisshead mates where he no doubt suffered the ignominy of them ribbing him about his son's apparent homosexuality. During his service in the Royal Air Force my father developed a passion for photography that he continued only sporadically once back on civvy street. I guess the call of the public house was too strong to ignore. When he became seriously ill he threw himself into his hobby turning the kitchen into a dark room and the lounge into a makeshift studio. What a shame that it took being diagnosed with a terminal medical condition to finally find some fulfilment from life.

'The saddest thing in life is wasted talent and the choices you make will shape your life forever.' Chazz Palminteri (Actor)
One evening I returned home from a training ride, it must have been sometime in May or June as school hadn't yet finished for summer but there was no sign of it going dark and it was still quite warm. I quickly stuck my head in the living room door on my way down the hall to let my mum who was watching television know I was back. As I put my bike away I wondered what my sister was doing home from university, anyway nothing to do with me so I carried on with my post ride routine. After almost ten minutes had passed my mother came into the kitchen and whispered conspiratorially 'there's a girl waiting for you in there.' I asked her who she is but all my mother knows is that she has come over from Shelley's. Shelley is another girl in my year at school who lives across the street, she is best friends with a girl called Joanna, that's who it must be.

Joanna and I end up having a relationship over the next eighteen months during which time cycling eventually became relegated to the back burner in favour of dates involving lots of heavy petting and alcohol fuelled nights out with friends. Besides any aspirations of one day becoming a pro were quickly relinquished when I realised how terribly difficult competitive cycling actually is. Cycling is the hardest sport there is, fact. Cycling is synonymous with suffering, you can possess all the talent and physical ability in the world but if you don't have the mental aptitude to suck it up and take the pain you might as well hang your wheels up.

In a sport consumed by stories of suffering and fortitude perhaps two of the severest are attributed to Tyler Hamilton, former key Lieutenant to Armstrong during the US Postal years. At the 2003 Tour Tyler was involved in a mass pile up on the very first stage of the race fracturing his collarbone. Rather than give up he managed to finish the race fourth overall stunning everyone with a memorable solo breakaway over 142km to win Stage 16. Only the year before at the Giro d'Italia he had broken his shoulder in a crash but incredibly finished second overall winning Stage 14 along the way, however he required extensive dental treatment after grinding down several teeth due to the extreme pain.

There may be tougher one day events such as the Ironman triathlon but no other sport puts such extreme physical demands on its participants for such extended periods. The paradox of cycling is that the hardships faced by the protagonists has itself been responsible for the doping problems that have plagued the sport. To become a successful cyclist requires you to live a pious, monastic existence where you need to be completely dedicated and focused on every aspect of your lifestyle.

EAT, BIKE, SLEEP, REPEAT being the pros mantra.

Having something of an addictive personality I had to honestly acknowledge that mentally as much as physically I didn't possess the qualities necessary to make it.

Something else had also been niggling at me for a while which made it easier for me to succumb to Joanna's charms and enjoy a hiatus from cycling. Over a period of time I'd begun to notice an attitude within the amateur sport that disappointed and angered me. I'll ride with anyone as long as I can keep up but to say cycling is cliquey would be an understatement. I've encountered riders who have looked down their nose at me without even seeing me ride just because I've been wearing professional team kit. A woman I used to work with years ago said she always knew it was me because I looked like a bag of skittles on a bike, this was back during my Mapei days. Mapei were another superteam that dominated the professional racing scene especially 'the Classics' during the 90s.

Floyd Landis, another former teammate of Armstrong who was stripped of his 2006 Tour win for providing a positive doping test for testosterone enjoyed similar experiences when he first started racing. He was raised in a very strict Mormon community in rural Pennsylvania and was actively discouraged by his father from taking part in cycling races. Floyd would sneak out of the house in the dead of night to go training so his father wouldn't find out he was being disobeyed. When he secretly attended a local amateur race on an old Schwinn bike wearing sandals and argyle socks the other competitors laughed and verbally abused him. He thought 'right I'll show you lot' and as soon as the flag dropped he rode them all off his wheel and won by a country mile.

I've never raced or ridden with a club ever since.

CHOOSE CYCLING, CHOOSE BEING A MAMIL, CHOOSE SUNDAY MORNING CLUB RUNS, COMPACT CHAINSETS, ELECTRONIC DERAILLEURS, TWENTY FIVE MIL TYRES AND DISC BRAKES. CHOOSE CHEAP IMPORTED CARBON FRAMESETS, DEEP SECTION AERO WHEELS, ENERGY GELS, MARGINAL GAINS AND COMPETING AGAINST FUCKING IDIOTS YOU'VE NEVER MET ON *STRAVA*. CHOOSE A SPORTIVE, POST RIDE MASSAGE AND WEARING A FINISHERS T-SHIRT. CHOOSE A POWER METER, CHOOSE A SPORTS WATCH, GET A BIKE FIT, WATCHING THE TOUR ON LIVESTREAM, POSTING PICTURES OF YOUR RIDE ON *INSTAGRAM* AND HOPING SOMEBODY GIVES A SHIT. CHOOSE RIPOFF DESIGNER CYCLING WEAR, LACE UP SHOES, CALF LENGTH SOCKS, SHAVING YOUR LEGS, CHAMOIS CREAMS AND PERINEUM FRIENDLY SADDLES. CHOOSE REALITY FUCKING BIKE RIDES ON *ZWIFT*, INTERVAL TRAINING, TURBO SESSIONS AND ACKNOWLEDGING OTHER RIDERS. **CHOOSE CYCLING.**

These Aren't the Droids You're Looking For

'Watching the wonderful Bicycle film was a great lesson in the history of the sport that has become my life and passion. I hope it can inspire more people to give cycling a go.'
Tracey Moseley (World Enduro Mountain Bike Champion 2013)

What is it that defines you?
Me?
I'm a cyclist and a biker (motorcyclist), I'm a husband (hopefully a good one) and a doggy daddy (again hopefully a good one) and a firefighter but before I became any of those things I was a son and a brother.

In our modern anti bullying society it won't come as a surprise to you to know that as a small child at primary school I was bullied by a much older and bigger boy called John Hudson, his only mistake being to choose a Greenwood as one of his victims. Eventually my mother prised it out of me as to why every Monday morning I seemed to develop a phantom poorly tummy in an attempt to not have to go to school. My father who himself was fond of a good scrap suggested that I should learn to fight my own battles but my mother and her protective maternal instinct were having none of it. I doubt she'd get away with it now but in the 1970s things were very different and like I've already mentioned everyone in the village knew who we were and of our reputation.

She stormed into the playground as the whole school were enjoying morning break and pinned the aforementioned lad against the wall grabbing him by the scruff of his neck and proceeded to, I'd say threaten but it wasn't a threat because she meant every word she said, reassure him that should he even look in my direction in a funny way she would give him a right good hiding! All the kids, even the teachers stood there open mouthed waiting for a reaction. You could have heard a pin drop. Turns out Master Hudson who was fond of calling the lollypop lady an '*old cow*' did actually possess the sense he was born with and managed to keep his mouth firmly shut.

He never came near me again.

Another boy was also being bullied but it wasn't by a fellow pupil, surprisingly it was by his own mother. Everyone knew when he'd been a naughty boy as she would drag him into school having dressed him up in a flowery summer frock leaving him to suffer the ridicule from the rest of the school. What became of him I don't know but I can only assume the experience has affected the rest of his life.

The only other time I was bullied was in high school and it was over a girl which came to a head one day on the bus home from school. The protagonist having the backing of his older brother and cronies proceeded to use his fists against me until my sister intervened. When my sister and I got off the bus I burst into tears because I was frustrated and angry not because he'd hurt me, in fact in a one on one situation I was pretty sure I could give as good as I got but he didn't have the minerals for that. My sister who was sitting her A levels that summer and would soon after be going off to university said to me ''There's only two things you should fight for in this world; somebody you love and something you believe in.'' Told you she was smart our kid.

When I were a lad there was no internet and social media, a mobile phone meant finding a red public telephone box and hoping that some wanker hadn't stolen the address directory. Nowadays if I have a mechanical or need assistance when I'm out cycling I just reach into my back pocket for my mobile and ring the wife to come pick me up but back when I started cycling it was a case of striking out for home on shanks pony until you found a phone box to reverse the charges for a mum cab. One such incident occurred many years ago in the Forest of Bowland, the roads were damp from light drizzle which caused me to lose the front wheel on a fast downhill approach to a sharp right bend leading to a bridge over the river. As I slid along the tarmac shredding skin the wall of the bridge filled my vision until both myself and the bike crashed into it with a sickening thump. A surge of adrenaline meant I didn't really recognise my injuries at the time but the front wheel was buckled and unrideable which led to a long walk to find the nearest phone box and an even longer wait to be rescued.

If you wanted to find something out you had to visit a library and actually read a book. Wi-fi and Bluetooth were unheard of whilst streaming and buffering were most likely to be associated with freak weather phenomenon. There was no satellite TV, I actually don't think there were any satellites and we only had four channels to choose from whilst computer games were very much in their infancy. If someone had told me then that a device would be invented that would fit in the palm of your hand which at the press of the button would give you access to all the information in the world whilst connecting you with virtually the rest of the human race I'd have told them that they'd been reading too many Philip K Dick novels or watching too much Star trek.

There was an invention however in the mid '70s that revolutionised our childhood and brought the world of movies into our living room. The video recorder meant that not only could you record programmes on television to watch again at your leisure but now there was no longer the requirement to go to a cinema to see the latest movie releases. Thus ensued a format war between Video Home System (VHS) and Betamax which soon became known to be of a lesser quality leading to VHS securing the majority share of the market. However it seemed everybody had that one friend whose father was the owner of an extensive porn collection on the Betamax format so we would all congregate at their house waiting for his parents to go out.

Our first VHS recorder was a beast of a machine, it took both my parents to carry it into the house and it would have been like being hit by a block of concrete had you the strength to throw it at someone. The machine was a top loader which sounded like the landing gear of a 747 being deployed when it was opened to insert a cassette. It also had a remote control, well as remote as the metre long cable it was attached to the machine by would allow. The most annoying things were that it seemed etiquette, no matter how poor, to not bother rewinding the cassette after viewing which meant a frustrating five minutes or more were wasted waiting to get back to the beginning of the movie. Also after the cassettes had been abused for a length of time the quality would decline with the recorder often seeming to develop a ravenous appetite for the internal ribbon resulting in complete picture distortion. The cassettes had a plastic tab which could be removed to safeguard any recordings made on it, however all you had to do was stick a piece of tape over and you were good to go. It wasn't uncommon to finish watching a movie to then find yourself viewing the first dance of somebody's wedding.

My first cinema experience was at the age of nearly seven when my sister and I went to see Star Wars: Episode IV- A New Hope, we felt so grown up being there on our own even though our parents were only in the screen next door watching Steven Spielberg's cult classic Jaws. I remember how vast the auditorium seemed and haven't felt an assault on the senses when the movie started the like of which until I visited the Bangla road in Phuket, Thailand. Everyone to a man in that theatre screamed with fear when the malevolent Darth Vader swept onto the screen for the very first time.

Pirate copies soon flooded the VHS market and it wasn't long before we acquired our own copy of both the aforementioned films. The picture and sound quality wasn't the best but we didn't care as we were transported to a different world of make believe. It wasn't long before it became part of our Saturday routine to have a matinee of one of those two movies and on rare occasions we managed to cram both in before the final football scores or wrestling came on, shouting 'Easy! Easy! Easy!' at the telly as Big Daddy overcame the beastly Giant Haystacks. I can say without hyperbole that we must have watched both those movies a thousand times to the point where we knew the scripts word for word and would assume the various characters voices throughout the films. Chewbacca and R2-D2 were particularly difficult ones to master.

In that period Hollywood seemed to produce an inordinately large number of horror movies many of which were so bad that they became known as 'B' movies. At some point or other I must have watched the majority of them from Friday 13th to The Evil Dead. One that has literally scarred me for life was John Carpenter's 'Hallowe'en' about a young boy who murders his entire family then twenty years later escapes the lunatic asylum where he has been incarcerated ever since to embark on a killing spree intent on finding and murdering his half-sister played by the demure Jamie Lee Curtis who is perhaps best remembered for revealing her magnificent breasts in 'Trading Places'. And I thought my family had issues. Why on earth my parents would encourage such a young child to watch movies like that is beyond my comprehension but they did. The soundtrack of the film alone freaked me out and my father knowing how traumatised I was by it would use this against me to *encourage* me to succumb to his will by playing the music as loudly as possible until I did as I was told.

A school mate from down the road called Martin started coming to our now legendary Saturday matinees and it was only after suffering nightmares following on from watching 'A Werewolf in London' that my mother received a telephone call from his giving her what for that stopped him coming anymore. The special effects were amazing for the time and it was wonderful to see a young Jenny Agutter both in and out of her nurses' uniform.

During the eighties a Hollywood blockbuster called Top Gun was released which in no time became a cult classic prompting the biggest recruitment drive the US Navy had experienced since the Second World War. The main character, super cool controversial flying ace Maverick played by Tom Cruise rode a Kawasaki Ninja which as an impressionable teenage lad reawakened my earliest desires for owning a motorcycle and reaffirmed to me that a military career was the way to go.

And that's how at eighteen I came to join the army which meant for a long while cycling became the furthest thing from my mind.

Baptism of Fire

'Cyclists see considerably more of this beautiful world than any other class of citizens. A good bicycle, well applied, will cure most ills this flesh is heir to.'
Dr K. K. Doty (19th century New Yorker and bicycling evangelist)

I never fell out of love with cycling, we were just on a break. Cycling is like having a best friend, you don't need to see each other that often but you know they are there should you need them and when you do meet up it's like nothing has changed. If anything until I met my wife cycling was the one constant reliable facet of my life that provided me with genuine pleasure and distraction from the mundanity and stress of modern life.

What is it I love about cycling? Love can be an emotion that is difficult to quantify and which can mean different things to different people but I'm fairly certain that there are many common denominators why people are drawn to cycling. I love the sense of freedom, the feeling of adventure and exploration. I love being outdoors, taking in the fresh air enjoying the surroundings. I've never been a gym bunny and don't really understand those vain people checking themselves out in the mirrored walls as they throw lumps of metal about. And as for spin classes well that's just retarded. I find cycling to be an escape where the stresses of everyday life are left far behind and a quiet time to think things through. Cycling is as good for your mental wellbeing as it is for your physical self. In fact most of this book has been 'written' in my head during the solitude of training rides. Also I believe there has to be something of a masochist in you to be a cyclist. There is a great deal of satisfaction from riding hard feeling that raw power coming from your body whilst enjoying an endorphin rush. I enjoy that visceral feeling of being fit. When I was in the Army I had to undergo a very thorough medical examination prior to undertaking the 'Selection Tests'. It was conducted by a Major from the RAMC (Royal Army Medical Corps) who wrote in the miscellaneous comments on his report four words; ***FIT FOR ARDUOUS TRAINING***. I've always enjoyed hard physical activity. The bottom line is that I just enjoy riding bikes, whether it has pedals or an engine if it has two wheels I'll happily ride it.

There aren't many things I don't enjoy about cycling but probably every cyclist nemesis has to be the wind. Studies have shown that over twenty percent of your energy can be wasted riding against the wind as basically you're just like a big sail sat on a bike. Where I live near the sea it's often windy which is great for resistance training but demoralising when you constantly feel like you are banging your head against a wall.

I'm also a fair weather cyclist but let me explain why I hate getting wet. The reason for this goes back to my childhood. My father was in the RAF before I was born and after he had discharged stayed friends with a comrade called Kev who lived in County Durham. We occasionally visited his family and during one such visit I was playing out with his son who was of a similar age to myself. There was a typically heavy summer downpour and by the time we'd made it back to the house we resembled a pair of drowned rats. My mother went absolutely berserk screaming and shouting like a Salford fish wife, anyone would have thought we'd broken the priceless family china. What an embarrassment. Not that we owned any priceless china, we were poor and working class something I'm as proud of as having bettered myself and being more successful than my parents. This sort of behaviour wasn't out of character for my mother, quite the contrary she has always had a habit of going off like a bottle of piss at the slightest thing. Now that I think about it I've never really worn a watch which I believe to be a subconscious decision due to the traumatic experience of being taught to tell the time by my mother who would scream and shout like a madwoman when I was unable to grasp the concept of minutes to the hour.

However perhaps what I like least is sharing the road with all the idiots out there. I've been cycling for over thirty years now and in that time I've seen how the volume of traffic has increased to levels that the road infrastructure is struggling to cope with not to mention the state of the roads which are shockingly bad and continually getting worse. The standards of driving in this country are absolutely terrible with cyclists suffering the effects of this. It boils down to road users having a lack of knowledge, training, experience and respect. This is why I love cycling on the continent because drivers are very respectful as cycling is part of the culture and almost everyone still rides a bicycle. Not only does there need to be a system of periodic retesting introduced but also drivers need to be educated to be respectful of more vulnerable road users. There should also be a progressive scale of proving competency as a road user, by this I suggest before you're allowed to drive a car you need to attain a recommended standard on a motorcycle and likewise to use a vehicle larger than an average sized car. This would give everyone a greater appreciation, awareness and knowledge of other road users. Finally there needs to be much harsher penalties for driving offences as people are literally getting away with murder. I appreciate that cyclists can sometimes be their own worst enemies but the absolute disrespect shown by the majority of motorists is completely unacceptable. Rant over!

You might have thought I'd have put crashing on my list of dislikes, don't get me wrong I don't want to crash but my philosophy has always been 'if you're not prepared to come off you shouldn't be riding.' I've had more than my fair share of crashes, some bad some innocuously embarrassing and some downright ridiculous such as the time I came to a stop and couldn't unclip out of the pedal quickly enough resulting in me falling over and the chainring slicing my ankle open. Perhaps the worst was when a car turned right across the carriageway in front of me when I was travelling at about twenty five miles per hour. The bike completely sheared in two upon impact as I was thrown over fifty feet down the road. And I wasn't wearing a helmet. I was rushed to hospital where I spent five days suffering with a severe concussion, if you've had concussion you'll know what a completely weird experience it is like you've taken some kind of hallucinogen, well I suppose your mind has quite literally expanded. The worst part though is that the hospital staff won't let you sleep in case you don't wake up. Nowadays I always wear a helmet.

After that very real near death experience I became convinced of having a guardian angel. I know who she is too, her name is Lena my maternal grandmother who sadly died prematurely in her forties of lung cancer. Her and Arthur junior my grandfather, had always wanted to have a son having been blessed with four daughters but Mother Nature only afforded them with the heartache of a stillborn son, Peter. My mother says the night I was born Lena was sat in the chair next to the bed with a great big beaming smile on her face.

There were a few periods during my twenties when I didn't touch a bike for months on end but then a certain American cancer survivor changed all that when he shocked the world of cycling by winning the 1999 Tour de France which came to be known at the time as the Tour of Redemption. There are certain athletes who transcend their sport, Muhammad Ali in boxing, David Beckham in football, Usain Bolt in athletics. These athletes have not only reached the very pinnacle of their chosen sport raising its profile to unimaginable heights but have actually become bigger than sport itself. Armstrong was destined to do the very same in professional cycling. For a short while at least.

The Texan Lance Armstrong was a successful triathlete by the age of sixteen who decided to concentrate on cycling eventually turning professional in 1992 at the age of twenty one for the American team Motorola. He had a rather inauspicious start finishing last in his first professional race but soon fulfilled his much vaunted potential with some notable victories including becoming the youngest ever World Champion on the road. He was young, ambitious and brash to the point of being arrogant which created many enemies within the pelotons traditionally respectful and hierarchical structure. In a very French sport the fact he all but refused to speak a word of the language didn't endure him to his peers or fans either.

In the autumn of 1996 he was diagnosed with testicular cancer which had spread to his abdomen, lungs and brain, the prognosis was that he was given less than a twenty percent chance of survival. After successful surgery and intensive chemotherapy treatment he was eventually given the all clear, however the cycling community had all but disowned him. During this period he created the Lance Armstrong Foundation charity to take on the battle against cancer which has raised millions of dollars and become synonymous with the yellow **LIVESTRONG** wristbands.

The reincarnation of Motorola, US Postal under the management of Johan Bruyneel, who became his co-conspirator in the biggest doping programme ever seen in sport, were the only team willing to take a chance on him. He returned to racing late in the 1998 season proving he'd lost none of his talent or determination by placing a remarkable fourth overall at the Vuelta a Espana (Tour of Spain) before going on to win the first of seven Tours the following year.

Lance pre cancer wasn't considered to be a grand Tour rider, all his success had been in one day races or week long stage races, his best finish in fact his only finish in four starts at the Tour was thirty sixth in 1995. He attributed his astounding performances to losing weight whilst suffering from cancer and subsequent sustained training in the high mountains. Following his Tour win Greg Lemond was moved to utter the infamous premonition 'If Lance is clean, it is the greatest comeback in the history of sports. If he isn't, it would be the greatest fraud.'

Armstrong became an inspiration to millions of fans myself included and I added it to my bucket list that I had to see him in action racing at the Tour.

When Lance won that first Tour I had just joined the civil service, where in the spring of 2001 I ended up befriending a colleague called Chris who not only happened to live just up the road from me but also happened to be a keen cyclist. Chris, a vegan is tall, wiry and very skinny. There's almost no fat on him whatsoever, I've actually seen more meat on a butcher's pencil. He has the build more becoming of a fell runner than a cyclist which makes me look almost obese next to him. He races the track during winter at the velodrome in Manchester and his claim to fame is that he once beat Olympic Sprint champion Jason Kenny in a race for the line. My cycling claim to fame is once riding with Alan Ramsbottom of Accrington who was one of the original pioneers of British cycling in the European peloton during the 1960s. He rode successfully on the continent for several years with high placings in the Ardennes Classics and finished sixteenth overall in the 1963 edition of the Tour de France.

Chris has that arrogant attitude I've experienced before and I no longer speak to him because of it. The first time we went cycling together before we'd even turned a wheel he said to me quite sincerely 'All the gear, no idea!' because I was dressed in full Mapei team kit. I can still vividly recall his reaction when I told him I'd got in 'the job'. Being in 'the job' is parlance used by members of the Fire Service which has its own language something a layman will never understand, much like how members of the special forces refer to their unit as 'The Regiment' and not the S A S. You'd have expected him to be overjoyed for me, far from it though in fact he almost turned green unlike his brother, already in the job, who was made up for me. The final straw came at the beginning of 2017 when he asked me what rides I had planned for the year. I told him that I was doing Liege-Bastogne-Liege but the 153km route and not the full leg destroying 272km distance. His response 'We'll make a proper cyclist of you one day!' really fucking pissed me off. I think after finishing two Roubaix I've more than qualified myself. However one of the best things he ever did was introduce me to a friend of his from his schooldays Alan, another fellow cyclist with whom I would develop a close and lasting friendship.

I'm proper jealous when I find out that Alan and Chris have planned a road trip to the Alps to watch the Tour and try not to show my envy when upon their return they regale me with tales of riding in the high mountains. We agree to go the following year which is how I find myself suffering a baptism of fire in the suffocating heat of Provence tackling perhaps one of the most infamous and difficult climbs in the whole of France the Mont Ventoux. We are riding the climb from the traditional south side leaving the village of Bedouin following the route that the Tour will use the day after. The climb is thirteen and a half miles in length gaining in excess of sixteen hundred metres of altitude!

During the 1967 Tour on the 13th July the race passed through the village taking in the Ventoux on the way to a stage finish in nearby Carpentras. Tom Simpson the greatest British cyclist ever and already a legend in the peloton was a serious contender for overall victory and determined to be one of the protagonists on such a crucial stage. In the lead group with only a few kilometres to the summit Simpson began to falter and started to zig zag across the road before falling off. Legend has it that Simpson uttered the ill-fated words *'Put me back on my bike'* to his mechanic in the following team car. He was helped to remount and rode on for a further few hundred metres before falling a second time only this time he didn't get up. Unconscious the prone Simpson was given medical treatment by the race doctor before being air lifted by helicopter from the mountain. He was pronounced dead at the nearby hospital in Avignon where empty vials of amphetamines were found in the pockets of his jersey, however cause of death was recorded as 'heart failure due to exhaustion.' A monument stands in the barren rock near the spot where Simpson collapsed which has become something of a shrine to cycling fans who leave all manner of cycling memorabilia in remembrance.

Leaving the village of Bedouin the climb starts gently enough as it passes through farmland and vineyards for a couple of kilometres leading me to naively think that this isn't so bad. However a left hand corner soon takes you into the trees where the gradient and the heat ramp up significantly, the Ventoux asserting her unwavering authority over you. Unlike other Cols the Ventoux is almost devoid of hairpin bends which has the effect of demoralising you as the road just seems to go on forever continually sapping the strength from your legs without the opportunity for a respite, albeit briefly to spin your legs through the hairpins. I've never experienced heat like this before whilst riding a bike, the sweat is absolutely pissing out of me and it's as though somebody is holding a running shower head over me. After several excruciating miles you emerge from the trees into what appears to be a lunar landscape at Chalet Reynard, a former refuge now restaurant. The final kilometres to the summit feel even harder, maybe that's due to fatigue or it could be the unrelenting heat radiated off the barren white limestone rock coupled with the constantly strong headwind. As cramp begins to grip my thighs I pass the Simpson memorial throwing a brief salute and struggle on upwards before finally taking the steep right hand bend up to the observatory at 1909 metres above sea level after almost two hours of continuous climbing. The French have a saying that 'You don't have to be mad to go up the Ventoux but you have to be mad to go back'.

The following day we return to the Ventoux and ride about half way up finding a good spot to await the arrival of the Tour, there are thousands of campervans, cyclists and fans doing exactly the same. About an hour before the race is due the Caravan passes through, this is a cavalcade of race sponsors using the opportunity to advertise their products, anything from foodstuffs to the national supermarket chain to watchmakers and more. As they pass the waiting crowd turns into an eager frenzied horde for the free souvenirs that are thrown at them by the people manning the Caravan. I end up with a gigantic green cardboard hand advertising the Points jersey competition which proves somewhat problematic to manage on the descent back to the campsite afterwards.

You can feel the anticipation building amongst the crowd like an electrical current, the helicopters hovering overhead signalling that the race isn't far away. It's like a scene from Apocalypse Now all that's missing is Wagner's Ride of the Valkyries playing over the loudspeaker. As the noise from above increases, almost as a single entity we the spectators move into the middle of the road craning our necks to get a glimpse of these warriors of the road. The French equivalent of 'CHIPS' part the crowd like Moses parting the Red sea as a small group of riders fly past. What astonishes me is the speed at which they are going compared to my tortoise like efforts of yesterday. Several minutes later Armstrong resplendent in the maillot jaune surrounded by the blue train of his US Postal teammates whizzes past in the blink of an eye, I'm rather disappointed that my first encounter with Big Tex is so fleetingly short. And just like that the Tour has gone. We've waited for several hours for just a few minutes of action. Was it worth it, you're damned right it was.

Two days later we're in the heart of the French Alps near the summit of the ski resort of Les Deux Alpes where during the 1998 Tour in atrocious weather Jan 'Der Kaiser' Ullrich the winner in 1997 who was renowned for disliking poor weather racing conditions capitulated to a long range attack by Marco Pantani which effectively cost him the race. Pantani was perhaps the last of the pure breed of climbers able to launch and sustain extremely aggressive attacks often taking minutes from his rivals. However 'Il Pirata' was also one of the unluckiest riders in the professional peloton who suffered numerous career threatening crashes even being taken down by a black cat crossing the road in front of him on one occasion. In an era of the sport riddled by doping although he never tested positive rumours were rife and when in an unassailable lead at the 1999 Giro d'Italia he was thrown off the race on the penultimate day for providing an excessively high blood haematocrit reading of 52%. Prior to a definitive and conclusive drug test for EPO being available riders were allowed a result of up to 50% red blood cells, anything higher was considered to be unnatural and attributed to EPO abuse resulting in a temporary suspension to safeguard the riders health. Being disqualified from his home race when he was set to win his second Giro ultimately proved to be the catalyst of his downward spiral from the very top of the sport when in February 2004 he was found dead in a Rimini hotel room of a cocaine overdose. Rumours and conspiracy theories abound about his death claiming Pantani was murdered and that the Mafia were involved although his death was officially recorded as accidental. Over twenty thousand mourners attended his funeral such was his revered status in Italy and amongst the cycling fraternity.

Today unlike in '98 the weather is glorious as we await the arrival of the Tour. Again it's all over in a flash with just a cursory glimpse of Armstrong who is content to simply defend his race lead and be chaperoned to the finish by his Postal teammates. We descend like madmen back down the mountain finding ourselves at the back of a large fast moving peloton on the flat roads heading to Bourg d'Oisans when a lad near the head of the line shouts 'There's a girl on the front ripping your legs off lads, you're not going to have that are you?' Don't ask me why but the red mist comes over me and I quickly move up through the group putting the hammer down as I hit the front. After a couple of minutes of full gas effort Chris moves past me to take his turn, I immediately jump on his wheel taking a welcome breather in his slipstream. We each take a couple more turns before I look over my shoulder to see that we have completely obliterated the group, even Alan hasn't managed to stay with us. We spin back to the campsite in the beautiful village of Allemont at the foot of the Col du Glandon Alan eventually catching us up.

That evening we are sat outside our tent enjoying the sunset and a couple of cold beers when we notice that the French lads in the tent next to ours, also a group of three are now down to two. Each morning as we have been preparing for the days ride, Bernard, Laurent and Jacques (we have named them after French Tour winners) have also been readying themselves for a day of riding and we have acknowledged each other with a cheery 'Bonjour, comment sa va?' However they wear body armour not lycra and ride downhill mountain bikes with huge front suspension forks and big knobbly tyres not lightweight racing bikes with skinny tyres. Bernard finally appears with a pot on his left arm from his fingers all the way up to his shoulder, oh dear he's in for an uncomfortable night.

On the final day in the mountains of my inaugural cycling road trip we ride back to Bourg d'Oisans to take on the legendary climb of Alpe d'Huez, famous for its twenty one hairpin bends named after Tour winners, which zig zag their way for over eight miles up to the ski resort summit at an altitude of 1860 metres. The Alpe was first introduced to the Tour in 1952 being won that year by Fausto Coppi, the bike he rode hangs in the local bike shop in town, and has been used almost every other year since. The mountain arguably attracts the most spectators of the whole race, almost half a million in 2015 with one of the hairpins now known as 'Dutch Corner' due to the hordes of Orangemen that congregate at the Notre Dame des Neiges church on race day. The lower slopes are incredibly steep which means getting into any kind of rhythm is an impossibility as I struggle to turn over the smallest gear I possess. As I climb higher the gradient eases off ever so slightly but the damage has already been done to my weary aching legs after several days of riding in the high mountains. Alan and Chris being much lighter and more adept at climbing have left me behind to my personal struggle with the mountain until I catch the wheel of a much older Italian rider. He has a mop of white hair which is even more striking against his deeply tanned skin, I'd guess he's in his late fifties, and is obviously in good nick given his athletic build. A couple of times I attempt to pass him but he's tapping out such a steady rhythm that I decide to instead sit on his wheel and get a bit of a tow. The Alpe really is a special climb, the views are spectacular as I've come to expect but the way the hairpins open up the climb means you can see for a great distance in front of you as well as where you have come from allowing you to admire the stunning mountain scenery. I've finally managed to give the old Italian boy the slip as I round the last couple of bends heading up through the resort and it's proliferation of bike, ski and outdoor shops towards the official Tour finish just below the altiport where my companions are waiting for me with satisfied smiles on their faces.

On the incessantly long journey back home to Blighty talk has already turned to next years' trip, Chris and Alan are keen to take on the Pyrenees having now visited the Alps twice. Suits me fine, I'm happy to just come along for the ride.

Four wheels move the body, two wheels move the soul.

I Predict a Riot

'There can be crowd issues everywhere in cycling. But it's a good thing for cycling that it's so accessible for spectators. That's why it's so popular - because fans can get close to the road and the race. But you also have to be aware of the dangers.'
Marianne Vos (Greatest female cyclist of all time)

July 2003
I'm flying! At least that's what it feels like, the sensation of speed heightened by the fact that the only contact between me and the road are two small patches of rubber less than an inch wide. We are hurtling down the descent of the Col d'Aspin in the French Pyrenees having safely negotiated the random herd of cows lollygagging about the summit when disaster almost strikes as my front wheel hits a large stone in the centre of the road. The bike shakes violently developing what is known in motorcycling parlance as a tank slapper and I almost shit myself. By the time I reach the safety of the valley I'm shaking like a shitting dog considering what the consequences of a high speed crash might have been especially to my weakened shoulder.

Only nine weeks previously I'd been involved in a very nasty road traffic collision where a total dickhead who hadn't bothered to indicate knocked me off my bike at an intersection causing me to break my collarbone, probably the most common injury suffered by cyclists. Let me tell you the pain was excruciating, I've never experienced anything so bad and hope I never will again. The last two months have probably been the most miserable of my life as I adjust to life being only able to use one arm and struggle to do everything with my non dominant hand. But silver lining to every cloud it did bring to an inevitable end a particularly unhealthy relationship. After the accident I didn't even think I'd make the trip but I did what all pros do when faced with a similar set of circumstances, hours of boring not to mention penile numbing turbo training sessions in an attempt to maintain my fitness.

The plan for the day had been to carry on and also ride the Tourmalet but after my near miss I make my nervous excuses to Alan and Chris swinging off into the campsite in the village of Sainte-Marie de Campan which has become our base for the week. The village and the mountain are steeped in Tour folklore when during the 1913 edition of the race whilst leading the race the Parisien Eugene Christophe walked over six miles down the mountain to the village after the forks on his bike had broken. When he eventually arrived in the village he located the local blacksmith where he set about welding his forks. The rules dictated that a rider was responsible for making his own repairs with assistance by a third party being strictly prohibited. It took him over three hours to fix his bike with a further ten minute time penalty added by the organisers for allowing the blacksmiths boy to work the bellows for him! Any chance of overall victory was gone and Christophe never did win the Tour. The Pyrenees were the first mountains ever to be used in the Tour when they were introduced in 1910 with the Tourmalet having more inclusions in the race since than any other climb. At the summit stands a remarkable silver statue of Octave Lapize, the first rider over the top in 1910 who infamously yelled at the organisers 'Vous etes des assassins! Oui des assassins!' as he passed them. It may be lost in translation as it definitely sounds better in French but what he said was 'You are murderers! Yes murderers!' Lapize went on to win the race that year, as well as being a triple winner of both Paris Roubaix and Paris Brussels during his career which was sadly curtailed when he was killed in 1917 during the First World War when as a fighter pilot in the French army he was fatally shot down.

The following day we ride across to the Col du Peyresourde for the first glimpse of that years' Tour locating a spot offering a commanding view of the whole mountain near the final hairpin less than a hundred metres from the summit. The second of four days in the Pyrenees was a tough stage tackling six catergorised climbs the final one being the Peyresourde before the descent to the finish in Loudenvielle. We can see the riders approaching from miles down the climb with a leading trio of Simoni, Virenque and the man himself Armstrong resplendent in the yellow jersey. This is by far the best view I've had of my hero and as he passes at the back of the group looks to be struggling to hold the wheel. I have enough time to look directly into his eyes which, blood shot red from the sustained effort stare transfixed into the distance. Then click everything comes back into focus, the noise of the crowd and the helicopters, the smell of exhaust gases and burning clutches from the following vehicles and the rush of air as the rest of the peloton whizz past millimetres from me.

Later that day Chris and I have a heated discussion over me using his spoon to stir my Heinz beans and sausage as I warm them in the pan. Chris being a vegan has taken umbrage at his cutlery being anywhere near a meat product and my argument that we are probably currently closer to a pig than these sausages have ever been doesn't seem to calm his rancour. As we're sat outside the tent enjoying the evening sunshine we are viciously attacked by a horsefly which looks like the insect equivalent of an Apache gunship. It dives in fast and low biting Chris on the ankle drawing blood before executing a hard right barrel turn to attack me also drawing blood from my knee. Alan is the bastards' final victim and he comes off the worst receiving a direct missile strike to his left hand. Within minutes his entire hand has swollen to over twice its normal size in an anaphylactic reaction, his skin resembling that of a very obese person which leads us to call him 'Fat Hand Al' for the rest of the trip.

Luz Ardiden with its ski station summit is our destination the next day as well as our last opportunity to see our heroes, these warriors of the road, as they battle it out in the high mountains. The dormant and seemingly docile crowd of which we are a part suddenly comes alive like a dragon awaking from its slumber as the Tour Caravan approaches. All of hell breaks loose, if it wasn't so funny it would be quite intimidating. Due to the close proximity of Luz Ardiden to the Spanish border means the crowd is more Spanish than French and to say the crowd is partisan would be an understatement. Unbeknownst to us the spot we have chosen is next to a group of young Spanish lads flying the colours of the Basque Country in various states of inebriation who have camped overnight on the mountain and spent all day drinking cheap red wine. There is also the sickly sweet stench of marijuana hanging in the air.

As the Tour cavalcade approaches through the mist one of our new friends disappears over a small knoll returning with a twenty litre bucket full of mountain spring water. What happens next is like the opening battle scene from the film Gladiator when Russell Crowe utters the command *'On my signal unleash Hell.'* As the first vehicle of the Caravan draws level with us our friend armed with the bucket full of water launches it all over the unsuspecting driver and passengers inside which is the catalyst for the others to throw everything they have at the other vehicles as they trundle past us at the speed of a funeral cortege. Every passing vehicle gets water boarded, our friend scurrying back and forth to refill his armoury like it's a version of that iconic game show of the '70's 'It's a Knockout' all he's missing is a ridiculously comedic clown like costume and Stuart Hall laughing his bollocks off in the background. Some bright spark from the advertising department for the French supermarket chain *Champion* has had the genius idea of creating a float resembling a market stall laden with actual real fruit and veg. The boys see this and like an amphetamine fuelled edition of 'Supermarket Sweep' strip the entire contents of the stall within seconds, a horde of locusts couldn't have done a better job. One lad has snatched a watermelon the size, and weight judging by the look of it, of a medicine ball which he proceeds to throw with all his might at the next passing car scoring a direct hit on the windscreen. Anyone within a five metre radius is instantly splattered in red juice, pulp and flesh. How on earth the windscreen didn't shatter is beyond me, yet the coup de grace is still to come.

I cross the road to chat with two English blokes in their late forties maybe even early fifties 'This is mental, isn't it!' I offer rhetorically. One of them replies matter of fact in a strong cockney accent 'It's just like a normal Saturday afternoon at a Millwall game.' As we're talking a French gendarme on a motorcycle crawls up the mountain out of the mist and as he passes us receives a full bucket of water soaking him to the skin from the chinstrap of his helmet to the top of his leather motorcycle boots. His bike stalls, plumes of steam billowing off the hot engine casing as he dismounts in search of the perpetrator. Eric Estrada looks as mad as a cut snake and seems to have murder on his mind his right hand reaching towards the butt of his service revolver holstered on his hip. A nervous quiet descends over the mob who like naughty schoolboys seem to realise they have gone one step too far this time. I swear on my father's grave though if Eric had pulled out that firearm he would have been lynched and thrown off the side of the mountain. Fortunately he seems to realise the odds are stacked against him, then giving us a stern wag of his finger remounts his bike managing to restart the engine after several attempts. He is seen off to much heckling and gesturing from the boisterous mob as the merriment spontaneously resumes. During my numerous visits to cycling races as a spectator I've never experienced anything like that day before or since. To be fair though our friends welcomed us warmly offering their wine as well as ammunition during 'the Battle of the Caravan' and cheerily waved us off with a hearty 'Adios' when the race had finished.

The helicopters hovering overhead and motorcycle outriders signal the arrival of the race with Armstrong off the front. He is out of the saddle going full gas in a flat out effort to distance his main rival Jan Ullrich. The 2003 Tour was the closest of Armstrong's victories with him only securing the win by just over a minute during the final time trial on the penultimate day. It could be argued that tactical ineptitude cost Ullrich a second Tour win rather than Armstrong's apparent loss of form which he later attributed to the effects of severe dehydration.

Jan Ullrich is perhaps the most talented grand tour rider to never really fulfil that potential only winning the Tour de France once in 1997 at the age of 23, although he finished second five times, and La Vuelta two years later. A strong climber and brilliant time trialist, he was World Time Trial champion in 1999 and 2001, he was a product of the strict sports programme from behind the Iron Curtain of East Germany so was not unaccustomed to the use of PEDs (performance enhancing drugs) and admitted to doping throughout his career several years after his retirement. During his racing career he was often struggling for form due to a lack of discipline in the off season and recurrent knee problems as well as a fondness for his mothers' baking and recreational drug use whilst enjoying the celebrity lifestyle.

Armstrong is bleeding from his left elbow, the yellow jersey ripped with abrasions to his shoulder, hip and knee. Our friends spit and throw urine at him as he flies past, to his credit he doesn't even flinch he's that far in the zone, again his eyes bloodshot red from the all-out attack. We later learn that on the lower slopes of the mountain whilst countering an attack by the Spanish hero Iban Mayo the handlebars of Armstrong's bike were snagged by a spectators' musette instantly bringing down both riders. In a remarkable display of bike handling Ullrich following the wheels managed to swerve the stricken riders. Incredibly neither rider was badly injured as the partisan crowd rush to the aid of their compatriot Mayo leaving Armstrong to fend for himself. The main protagonists appeared to attack the vulnerable race leader who almost crashed a second time due to damage sustained to his bike until Armstrong's fellow American and ex-teammate Tyler Hamilton called a truce at the head of the race allowing Armstrong to regroup. Once Armstrong had recovered he went on to launch the race winning move no doubt leaving his rivals to ponder what might have been.

Professional cycling is full of unwritten rules and strictly adhered to etiquette, one of which is that the race leader cannot be attacked if he has suffered a crash or mechanical issue. Of course such rules are open to interpretation and can cause controversy such as on Stage 12 of the 2016 Tour when due to heavy crowds near the summit finish on the Ventoux a crash brought down the race leaders including yellow jersey wearer Chris Froome. Bauke Mollema avoided the crash and attacked winning the stage by over a minute and a half whilst Froome, his bike badly damaged and unrideable started to run up the Ventoux on foot before assistance from the following team car eventually arrived. A protest was launched by Team Sky resulting in Froome being afforded the same time as the stage winner despite another rule that states using any other means of transport than a bicycle is forbidden.

Thinking back that Pyrenean trip of 2003 is my favourite of all the ones I made. Also it transpires that this was to be the last trip Chris would join us on as he entered the man made prison known as marriage later that year. Alan would be good for another three years before he too had the ball and chain fitted which left me flying solo in 2007 when I visited the Alps, the Ventoux and the Pyrenees revisiting some old enemies as well as tackling some of the more notable climbs from Lance Armstrong's illustrious Tour career.

In those six years I've ridden most of the major climbs that feature in the Tour as well as several lesser known ones and I can say with complete sincerity that there are no easy climbs in the high mountains and anyone who claims to the contrary is wrong. If I had to offer my opinion as to the hardest of all the ones I've ridden I would say it is undoubtedly the Ventoux due to the length, steepness and elevation gain as well as the conditions faced. The most enjoyable for me has to be Pla d'Adet in the Pyrenees simply because the scenery is absolutely stunning whilst I'd suggest the least difficult to be the Col du Telegraphe if it's ridden by itself and not as a precursor to the Galibier.

From those early teenage years when I first became infatuated with cycling there is one race that has captured my imagination as much as if not more so than the Tour de France.

That race is Paris Roubaix aka 'the Hell of the North', aka 'the Queen of the Classics', aka 'a Sunday in Hell'.

The Hell of the North

'Paris Roubaix is a horrible race to ride but the most beautiful one to win.'
Sean Kelly (race winner 1984 and 1986)

It's a common misconception that Paris Roubaix was given the nickname 'the hell of the north' because of how brutal the race is and the hardships facing the competitors in riding it. However apt the nickname may be sadly this is not the reason why.

After the First World War finished people were eager for life to return to normal and in early 1919 the organisers of the race made a reconnaissance of the route to see if it was possible to stage the race. What they found after four years of trench warfare and unrelenting shell bombardments came as quite a shock. The land had been completely pulverised into a bleak wasteland. Gone were all signs of life, the trees and any kind of vegetation had been replaced by a barren muddy featureless landscape littered with shell holes like an adolescents acne ridden face. The desolation encountered prompted one of them to utter the now infamous words that they had witnessed 'the hell of the north' and so the nickname was born.

Paris Roubaix was first held in 1896 and is the second oldest professional bike race still in existence. Liege Bastogne Liege aka La Doyenne ('the old Lady') is the only race older than it being first run in 1892. Both of these races make up part of the Spring Classics and both are known as 'Monuments' these are generally considered the oldest, hardest and most prestigious one day events in cycling. There are five 'Monuments' in all, the others being Milan San Remo (La Primavera- the Spring), Ronde van Vlaanderen (Tour of Flanders) and the 'race of the falling leaves' Giro di Lombardia. A win in any of these events will make a cyclists career.

Paris Roubaix is also known as the 'Queen of the Classics' in deference to its status amongst its peers, much as the longest, hardest and most mountainous stage of a Grand Tour will be called the 'Queen stage'. It may not be the longest, that accolade certainly goes to La Primavera aka Milan San Remo, it may or may not be the hardest, general consensus seems to err towards La Doyenne and given that it's relatively flat it certainly isn't the hilliest this being either De Ronde but most likely La Doyenne. Despite this it has earnt something of a mythical status becoming perhaps the most iconic and prestigious race on the calendar.

The race was the brainchild of a pair of textile magnates from Roubaix, Theodore Vienne and Maurice Perez. Both rich and keen cyclists they shared a desire to promote competitive cycle races so built a velodrome in 1895 where several meetings were held. As most road races at the time either started or finished in Paris and Roubaix was viewed as something of a backwater they cannily enlisted the help of Le Velo, Frances number one sports newspaper based in Paris which used sports events to promote itself, to organise the start of the race. On Sunday 19th April 1896 the first edition of Paris Roubaix was run over 280 kilometres finishing at their velodrome with prize money equivalent to that of seven months wages of a miner going to the winner Josef Fischer of Germany.

Nowadays there's still the velodrome finish but the winner receives a cobblestone mounted on a wooden plinth.

The early editions of the race were all mostly on cobbled roads as that's how all roads were constructed at the time. It wasn't until after the Second World War that improvements to the road infrastructure were made and the use of tarmacadam became more widespread, because of this many of the cobbled sections were being lost. Another factor was races were beginning to be followed by live television and Mayors of towns the race passed through didn't want their backyards looking like they lived in the dark ages so began resurfacing the cobbles in earnest. This prompted the organisers during the late 1960s to seek out old tracks and abandoned roads which have now come to characterize the race and form the basis of the route as it is known today.

Since 1977 the race has started from Compiegne, some 80 kilometres north of Paris with the first secteur of pave coming after 100km of riding in the area just outside of Busigny. The next 150km are littered with up to 29 secteurs of pave totalling in excess of 50km of riding on cobbles. These secteurs are graded according to the length, irregularity, general condition and position which might affect the race. A two star secteur being the easiest with five stars awarded to the hardest secteurs of the race. The route may be altered slightly from year to year if older roads are resurfaced or become too dangerous to use or if new secteurs are found which complement the race.

There are three 5 star secteurs included in the race at Mons-en-Pevele, Carrefour de l'Arbre and the infamous Trouee d'Arenberg which has come to symbolise the race.

Until 1990 Arenberg had a working mine and it was an ex miner turned professional cyclist Jean Stablinski who proposed the use of the Trench of Arenberg to the race organisers. Its first inclusion in the race was in 1968 and it has been used almost every year since. The pave here dates back to the Napoleonic era, it cuts straight through the forest at Saint-Armand-Wallers for 2.4 kilometres and is extremely difficult to ride due to its irregularity caused by subsidence from mining. For these reasons despite it being a considerable distance from the finish at Roubaix with many more secteurs of pave to negotiate it's considered a crucial stage of the race. As Stablinski himself said 'Paris Roubaix is not won in Arenberg, but from there the group with the winners is selected.'

Mons-en-Pevele has been used since 1978. It is a 3 kilometre secteur of extremely difficult pave to ride which comes about 50km from the finish and can prove crucial in the final selection for victory.

At 2.1km Carrefour de l'Arbre is the last and shortest five star secteur with arguably the least irregular pave of the three to ride. However it comes at a critical juncture of the race due to its close proximity to Roubaix, with only two more secteurs to go after it, when many riders have no legs left that race winning moves are often made here.

The final one star secteur is a mere sideshow after what's gone before and is a kind of ceremonial procession to the doorstep of the Roubaix Velodrome. In 1996 a brand new, smooth 300 metre long secteur was created on the Avenue Roger Salengro with the names of all the previous winners etched into the cobbles.

Saving the best until last is the final lap and a half of the velodrome itself. The original velodrome built by Vienne and Perez was used only until 1914 with the new Roubaix Velodrome on the Avenue Alexander Fleming hosting the finish from 1943 to the present day. In cycling terms it's something of a Holy Grail, a Mecca, like Wembley is to the FA Cup final, to finish at the velodrome is like finishing on hallowed ground.

The weather can also play a critical factor in the outcome of the race. Roubaix has become notorious for dishing up appalling weather which can make the pave absolutely treacherous to ride. In the dry the secteurs are extremely dusty, in the wet they become a quagmire of slick greasy mud. Spectators are used to seeing the riders with faces barely discernible as the whites of their eyes peer out from a mask of mud and grime. In recent years however most editions have remained dry which many purists believe has detracted from the value of the race.

Another facet of the folklore and legend happens after the race has actually finished when riders head for the iconic shower block to wash away the dust and grime from the hell of the north. The concrete three sided stalls are labelled with a brass plaque carrying the name of a former winner and resemble cow shed milking stalls. I suppose it's rather appropriate that the shower facilities offered are so basic reflecting the brutal journey to reach them.

The race also acquired another nickname in 1976 when a documentary was made by Jorgen Leth of Denmark entitled 'A Sunday in Hell'. The film has amongst the cycling fraternity acquired something of a cult status and follows the race and its main protagonists capturing the atmosphere of the race not just of the riders but also from the perspective of the spectators.

Also unique to this race is a group of enthusiastic volunteers called 'Les Amis de Paris Roubaix' (the friends of the race) founded in 1983 by Jean Claude Vallaeys. Its primary purpose was to save the cobbles and preserve the heritage of the race as many roads were being resurfaced. Today it focuses on maintaining and restoring the cobbles, yet despite their best efforts several secteurs have still been lost as they have deteriorated beyond repair.

However the race organisers are always on the lookout for new secteurs and indeed two new ones were added to the route in 2017.

As happens during the course of time in virtually all sporting events are tales of heroes and glory, misfortune, intrigue and scandal. A race that is over a hundred years old has more than its fair share of memorable moments. Most recently at the 2016 edition, Fabian 'Spartacus' Cancellara one of the greatest riders of the pave and race winner three times, rather ignominiously fell off his bike during his retirement lap of honour of the velodrome.

Who can forget the media furore the year before after many riders had taken enormous personal risk to carry on at a railway level crossing as the gates were closing, moments later a train barrelled through at high speed. This wasn't the first controversy involving a railway crossing however, back in 2006 three riders who were fighting for second place did exactly the same and were subsequently disqualified upon arrival at the finish (no riders were disqualified in 2015). This prompted one of the trio the Belgian classics specialist Peter Van Petegem and race winner in 2003 to comment 'It's crazy, in Belgium the train would have been stopped'.

Possibly the biggest scandal came in 1949 when the winner Andre Mahe was misdirected by officials which led to him entering the velodrome by the wrong entrance which meant he rode only a single lap and not the obligatory lap and a half. Serse Coppi, the younger brother of Fausto Coppi 'Il Campanissimo' (champion of champions) won the sprint for second place and subsequently entered a protest. It is alleged that Fausto told the organisers he would never ride their races again unless his brother was accredited the win so to appease him the result was declared a dead heat with Mahe and Coppi S. both recorded as the winner.

The race is often littered with crashes probably the most horrendous befalling Belgian Johan Museeuws in the Trouee d'Arenberg in 1998 which shattered his kneecap. Gangrene later set in and he almost had to have the leg amputated. Unlike Philippe Gaumont who suffered a similar fate, Johan eventually returned to professional cycling and won his second Paris Roubaix with a spectacular solo break in 2000. As he approached the finish line he took his foot out of the pedal and lifting his leg left pointed to his knee as a reminder of the almost career ending injury. He went on to win again in 2002 to match his three wins at De Ronde and quite rightly is affectionately known by his countrymen as 'the Lion of Flanders'.

The best result by a British rider was for many years by Barry Hoban in 1972 with a third place finish. This was equalled in 2004 by cyclocross specialist Roger Hammond and again in 2016 when one of my favourite riders Ian 'Yogi' Stannard of Team Sky found himself in a five man break including the Belgian pave specialist and four time winner Tom Boonen.

One might argue that in that same year when Roger Hammond stood on the podium Britain actually earnt its' first Roubaix victory with the Swedish rider Magnus Backstedt winning the sprint for the line. Standing at 6 feet 4 and weighing 90 kilos Magnus was a brute of a rider in the Viking tradition but living in Britain being married to a British girl with British children he had become an adopted son in the truest sense of the word.

Stannard earnt the nickname Yogi because he's a big friendly bear but also like a bear incredibly strong and aggressive on the bike. Probably Yogis most notable victory came at the Belgian semi classic Omloop Het Nieuwsblad in 2015 when in a four man break with yet again Boonen and three of his teammates Yogi continually resisted their attacks before he simply rode them all off his wheel in an amazing display of raw power. The saying goes that a picture paints a thousand words, well Boonens shake of the head as he crossed the finish line did exactly that. Our friends' daughter also babysits for Yogi so according to the law of six degrees of separation that practically makes us riding partners.

Boonen was hoping to take his fifth win thereby usurping 'Monsieur Roubaix' himself, Roger de Vlaeminck who also won four editions in the 1970s, and was undoubtedly the favourite to win but it seems his attacking riding during the latter part of the race left him devoid of energy and he was outsprinted to the line by fifteen year journeyman pro Matt Hayman of Australia, a very worthy and welcome winner with Stannard finishing third behind Boonen.

In 2011 the Paris Roubaix Challenge was introduced. The Challenge is an amateur sportive and is held on Saturday the day before the professional race is run on Sunday. There are three routes to choose from for a very reasonable price, the full unadulterated 172km which starts in Busigny and takes on the very same course and every secteur of pave the pros will race; a slightly shorter 145km route which starts and finishes at the velodrome in Roubaix but *only* takes in 18 secteurs beginning with a baptism of fire at the Trouee d'Arenberg or a shorter 70km version for the fainthearted which again starts and finishes at the velodrome but ventures over only the last seven secteurs however it does include the final five star secteur at Carrefour de l'Arbre. The brave or perhaps foolhardy competitors choosing the full distance are transported by coach with their bikes to the start in Busigny.

The event has become extremely popular attracting some four and a half thousand amateurs from all over the world eager to follow in the cycle tracks of their heroes. It is estimated that almost a third of all those taking part are from Britain whilst some lunatic has even attempted the short course on a Penny Farthing!

Dawgs, Dya Like Dawgs?

'Like dogs, bicycles are social catalysts that attract a superior category of people.'
Chip Brown (Writer/Journalist)

Well the simple and brutally honest answer to that question is no I didn't like dogs, that is until I met my wife Christine.

When I was growing up the only pets we had were two scruffy guinea pigs, their ears half chewed from fighting with the other little piggies, bought from a grotty back street pet shop in Bolton where it was possible to purchase what seemed like any animal imaginable aside from the African big five. Turns out one of them was gestating which meant we surprisingly ended up with several little pigs, most of which we gave away keeping just one of the litter. The matriarch of the group, Melissa was a rather grumpy sow but absolutely adored my mother. She was completely disinterested in anyone else but would become extremely excitable at my mother's presence.

My parents have never mentioned having pets as children which doesn't surprise me given their upbringing and there is absolutely no way my father would have been allowed to own a dog. My grandfather Joseph, known as 'Burma Joe' to his friends had been a Petty Officer in the Royal Navy aboard the battleship HMS Exeter during the Second World War. The Exeter was extensively damaged during the famous Battle of River Plate in the south Atlantic against the notorious German pocket battleship Admiral Graf Spee. Following repair the Exeter was ordered to the Far East where she was sunk during the Second Battle of the Java Sea and although most of the crew survived they were captured by the Japanese army suffering over three years of living hell as prisoners of war. Dogs were used to intimidate prisoners as well as being chased by them facilitating their capture when the crew first reached shore. The only two things he abhorred were the Japs and dogs. My sister and I occasionally stayed with my father's aunt who had two white miniature poodles which she completely molly coddled and were really annoying yappy little things which I think also put me off dogs. I hated those two little spoilt brats.

We also used to feed a stray cat which seemed to have made the coal shed in our back yard its home and appeared quite happy living outdoors, my mother is allergic to cats so there was never a chance of turning him into a house cat even if he'd wanted to. I don't think this can be classed as my first venture into animal rescue as the cat was never actually saved from the streets. But now that I think about it that actually came at about the age of eight. I remember being awoken one morning by a persistent scratching sound interspersed with the occasional high pitched chirp. On investigating the source of the annoying cacophony which had interrupted my sleep I found the noise to be coming from inside the window casing. Sparrows had a habit of building their nests within the eaves of our house and when my father opened up the window casing we found a young sparrow chick had fallen from the sanctuary of the nest. Unable to decide what to do with the chick we constructed a make shift nest using a shoe box full of tissue and cotton wool so we could transport it to a local bird sanctuary on the outskirts of Bury. I remember being completely amazed by the plethora of birds of prey in the shelter especially a pristine snow white faced Barn Owl that was able to completely rotate its head on its shoulders.

For some reason we ended up taking Frank the sparrow back home with us, if we had rescued him today no doubt we'd have called him Jack. He spent several weeks in our airing cupboard where it was warm and cosy being hand reared which consisted of feeding him live maggots procured from the local fishing tackle shop. Several weeks passed during which I watched with curious fascination as Frank grew from a chick to a fledgling eventually finding his wings by learning to fly in our kitchen signalling it was time to release him back into the wild. We made quite a ceremony of it as we took him outside in his cardboard box of a nest which had been his temporary home since we rescued him. We all went back inside and watched from the window as he became accustomed to his surroundings. He hopped about on the window ledge for a few minutes seeming to muster the courage then took flight and was gone, I cried. A few weeks later I was sat at the dining room table when there was a tapping sound behind me at the window, you can imagine my complete surprise when I turned round and there on the windowsill was a sparrow. Tap tap. Tap tap. I swear on my mother's life that it was Frank who'd returned to let us know that he was ok. I looked into his beady black eyes seeing the acknowledgement there then for the second time only this time forever he flew away. True story that.

It also seems ironically coincidental now that my Auntie Elizabeth owned an ex racing greyhound called Sandy, a fawn, dead original name I know but who was obviously an astute judge of character. He didn't like my father and would often follow him to the toilet on our visits to their house not letting him out again much to everyone's amusement.

These experiences have convinced me that all animals no matter the size of their grey matter are sentient creatures and have the capacity to feel emotions in exactly the same way human beings do.

'When I look into the eyes of an animal, I do not see an animal. I see a living being. I see a friend. I feel a soul.' A.D. Williams (author)

If it hadn't been for Tim Berners-Lee my wife and I would never have met each other, without his invention of the World Wide Web there would never have been a certain dating website to instigate our coming together. When we first met in June 2010 my wife was the proud owner of a ten year old pedigree male Weimaraner called Jack who was her big silver boy. I only know what a Weimaraner is because of the cult music video Blue Monday by eighties electropop band New Order pioneers of the Manchester music scene.

Originally bred in Germany in the 19th century for Grand Duke Karl August of Weimar as a gundog they were used for hunting large game consequently possessing a high prey drive and high energy levels. Other common breed traits are that they can be quite a handful due to the mental stimulation they require, can be stubborn and resentful of discipline as well as their need for constant companionship. Weimaraners are a large muscular athletic breed having a distinctive appearance with a silver-grey sleek short haired coat standing at over two feet tall and weighing up to forty kilograms. Traditionally the tail was docked as a puppy although this practice was banned in the United Kingdom under the Animal Welfare Act 2006.

It's fair to say that when Jack and I eventually met he was more keen to make friends than I was almost to the point where the more disinterested I was the more persistent he became in gaining my attention. Having never been around dogs before as well as being quite particular about my personal appearance I wasn't exactly comfortable with Jack's willingness to share his saliva and body hair with me. Over time as we became accustomed to each another I began to come to understand the pleasure and fulfilment that having a dog in your life can bring.

Before I'd always been of the opinion that dogs were needy, smelly and not particularly resourceful creatures unlike their feline counterparts and although elements of that may still be true there are so many enriching aspects to dog ownership. Something else which had previously bothered me about dogs were the owners themselves, those who treat their animals like small children talking to them in ridiculous voices, kissing, cuddling and pampering them. Also, have you ever noticed how many owners and their dogs look remarkably like each other, whether this a sub conscious decision when choosing a dog by the owner or whether it's a subliminal process due to the emotional attachment I'm not entirely sure.

Jack was born on the 18th May 1999 one of a litter of six, all male bred by Mrs Johnson of Airdrie, Scotland. His pedigree name was Silver Arron of Robston coming from a very distinguished bloodline called Gunalt which has won many show awards. Jack was a very handsome dog the only physical flaws being a couple of benign almond shaped lumps down his flanks that Weimaraners as a breed are prone to, I've seen some hideous ones so I suppose his weren't too bad. They can be removed but it's an unnecessary surgery for purely aesthetic reasons. As you'd expect from a hunting dog he was incredibly fit which probably explains why he lived to the ripe old age of fourteen. During his formative years he'd spent many a 'hunting' trip in the Scottish wilds with Chriss's ex-partner whose parents lived north of the border. She's told me how on visits there'd often be a bath tub full of salmon or a deer carcass hanging in the shed which Jack had helped catch often being fed the animals entrails as a reward.

It's the nature of the breed that Weimaraners don't enjoy being alone so when Chriss was at work Jack would go to her mums house. During our courtship as I spent more and more time at the house where I now live I became responsible for Jacks doggy day care needs. I remember at the beginning Chriss telling me that Jack had separation anxiety issues which to be honest I thought was complete codswallop. One afternoon I wanted to watch a film in peace so shut Jack in the dining room, all was quiet for about a millisecond before he started howling, crying and scratching furiously at the door. He was visibly relieved when I opened the door which made me feel somewhat guilty. I guess she was right.

Jack loved his walks and would happily roam for hours on the beach or in the hills on our frequent trips to the Lake District. Despite being a hunting dog he never bothered the livestock so we were able to let him off lead wherever we took him. He also loved his food but don't most dogs. Maybe it was the Jock in him but what he loved most was a beer, I swear that dog could hear the ring pull on a can of Stella from a mile away. I used to give him the frothy dregs from the can which he'd lap up with relish. We have a lovely garden which is perfect for sitting out in on the odd occasion when the weather is good. On a glorious summer's day Chriss and I were enjoying a few beverages as we sat out enjoying the sun and accidently ended up getting Jack pissed. I know how irresponsible it was but we hadn't realised how many cans we'd consumed giving Jack the dregs from each one, he didn't seem to mind even though he was a bit unsteady on his feet.

Over the years we formed a very strong bond becoming the best of buddies, although Chriss was always his favourite as he'd been with her since he was a puppy. The only things about him that irritated me were the amount of excrement he produced, I swear that dog could shit for England and how every time I moved he was up wanting to know what was happening. Weimaraners are known as the 'Silver Shadow' for their need to be at your side and follow you everywhere.

However time was against us as he entered his twilight years and even though he was willing mentally he was noticeably slowing down physically, then he had an episode which ultimately proved to be the beginning of the end. He was upstairs in the master bedroom lying on the sheepskin rug in the sunlight, one of his favourite places to relax whilst I was sat at the dining room table using the laptop just as I am now as I write this. If I look to the right I can see the wall mounted clock which I remember doing that day thinking that it was almost time for his dinner and that I'd go up and get him in a minute. No sooner had I checked the time than a banging noise started. I could tell from the sound that it wasn't somebody at the door but went to check anyway, of course there was nobody there. I checked outside, no obvious signs of the source of the noise but as I approached the foot of the stairs the noise became louder. For some reason I cautiously climbed the stairs fearing an intruder yet full well knowing there wouldn't be one all the time the banging becoming louder. The racket was coming from our bedroom.

Oh fuck no! Oh for fucks sake!

The banging noise was the sound of Jack's hind legs kicking the wardrobe as he struggled to get up, his eyes wide with fear. His bowels had let go which instantly made me think he'd suffered some kind of seizure. The strangest thing is the excrement didn't smell and we have all experienced how horrendous dog shit smells. I immediately dropped to my knees attempting to scoop him up so I could move him downstairs to make him more comfortable but he seemed to resist and struggle even more. There wasn't a great deal of space to manoeuvre between the bed and the wardrobe and with him fighting against me it was making the task almost impossible. I'm a reasonably strong, fit guy but trying to lift a forty kilogram weight that is working against you in a confined space was proving rather difficult. After a couple of attempts I managed to get a good grip of him and started for the stairs, as we descended his bowels let go again all over me. I tried not to notice. He began struggling with more effort when we entered the dining room where his bed was and he ended up slipping from my arms like a wet fish. I almost caught him with my knees before he hit the deck his bladder spontaneously letting go. I'm sorry to say I left him a puddle of his own piss as I grabbed my mobile to phone Chriss.

'C'mon, c'mon for fucks sake answer the fucking phone!' I shouted to nobody as the phone started to ring.

My wife's voice filled my ear 'Good morning the Great Hall'.

'Chriss, its Jack he's……..fuck…..you need to come home!' I hurriedly tell her trying to sound calm knowing that I sound anything but.

'I'm on my way' and before I can say any more the phone goes dead.

I manage to move Jack to his bed by a process of undignified sliding then lifting him into it, thank god for laminate floors. My attempts to soothe him seem to have no effect as he pants uncontrollably and his eyes remain wild with fear. In light traffic it is only a ten minute journey to where my wife works but that ten minutes seems to last forever. Finally I hear the front door open and as she enters the room Jack seems to calm considerably, I'm more than happy to let her take over. After several minutes although he appears a lot calmer he again starts struggling to stand up seeming to become more agitated at being unable to do so. Chriss asks for a large towel which we place under his midriff as a makeshift support helping him to his feet. Within an hour or so of helping him about to get a drink, go outside for a wee then back and forth to his bed he seems to make what is almost a miraculous recovery.

I can say with complete certainty that the traumatic events of that day will never be erased from my memory, neither will the guilt I've carried since that maybe if I'd gone upstairs earlier I could have prevented the whole episode.

We both knew that his days were numbered and this may sound terrible but I hoped that I would get up one morning and go downstairs to find he'd passed away peacefully in his sleep. He was stubborn though, aren't all Weimaraners, greeting me every morning with a smile and a wag of his tail or stump as it was. I also believe that he didn't want to leave us and the happy life that he had.

When my wife eventually shared with me the decision she'd reached to have him put to sleep I didn't object. Jack wasn't my dog after all, besides I'm fairly confident that I couldn't have reconciled that decision with my conscience if I'd had to make it. But she is a lot stronger than I am. His mind was still willing but his body was failing him, I remember one of the last walks we took together we only made it round the block and I thought I was going to have to carry him back the last stretch. There was an old lady out walking her little dog who commented as we laboured past 'He looks worn out.' I replied 'When you get to his age I'm sure you'll feel the same.'

When the final curtain call came Jack seemed to know, animals are far more attuned to their senses than we are, as he became rather agitated at going in the car something which had never bothered him before. The vets had stayed open late for us so that the place would be empty and they handled the situation with great care, respect and empathy. We were ushered into the examination room where we finally managed to settle Jack so they could begin administering the lethal injection but first they gave him a sedative to calm him down. I felt like a sedative myself but they weren't forthcoming in offering one. After about five minutes his breathing started to slow and we were asked if we wanted to stay to the very end. I'm sorry but that would have been just too heartbreaking to bear so we said our final goodbyes. I stroked his silver head and kissed him for the last time telling him I loved him.

Then we left.

The car was parked about ten paces from the front door of the practice and we just about made it before we both broke down sobbing uncontrollably. It still chokes me up now reliving those memories and I often ride pass the vets which always makes me think of that dreadful day. How could it affect me so much it's just a fucking dog it's not like we'd lost a child. But that's exactly what it was like, it was *just* like that.

I'm sorry Jack, we love you. Run free Silver Boy.

Tell me it's 'just a dog' and I'll tell you that you're 'just an idiot.'

Adopt Don't Shop

'Nature loves bicycles because no harm to Nature comes from the bicycle.'
Mehmet Murat ildan (Playwright and novelist)

The house seems incredibly quiet without Jack. Not that he was a noisy dog, actually he didn't bark very often and wasn't any trouble at all really. I don't miss the walks so much as I get enough exercise cycling but I do miss the companionship. He was my best buddy after all.

Several weeks pass by before my wife tells me she wants another dog. To be honest I'm not that keen on the idea for a number of reasons mainly because I know the future will eventually bring more heartbreak. But as happens in most relationships between a man and a woman for the sake of keeping her happy a man tends to let her get what she wants.

In this case my only unwavering stipulation is that we get a rescue dog as there is absolutely no way I'm going to pay hundreds of pounds for a puppy to some unscrupulous breeder looking to make a quick buck when there's so many unwanted dogs in rescue centres. The next conversation is about what kind of dog we are going to get, I've always been fond of sausage dogs but my wife quickly poo poos this idea, no pun intended, saying I'll look a right fairy walking that on Blackpool prom. Great Danes are another breed that we both like but when my wife contacts a Dane specific rescue we are quickly rebuffed on the grounds that we have never previously had ownership experience of one. We find out that this isn't an uncommon approach used by many breed specific rescues, little wonder then that there are so many dogs left on the shelf.

However what we find most disconcerting is the large number of rescue sites coupled with the enormous numbers of dogs available on each site. The numbers are absolutely staggering with breeds such as Staffordshire Bull terriers amongst the most popular or maybe that should be most unpopular. And to all those people who only want a puppy there's a proliferation of them available, it's not just older dogs. In my opinion there needs to be much tighter controls overseeing the breeding process to an extent where until the numbers of animals languishing in rescues are brought down to manageable levels breeding ceases unless the animals are to be used for strictly working purposes. Don't even get me started on those idiots that spend a fortune on a designer mongrel or those stupid celebrities with their ridiculous handbag dogs which only perpetuates over breeding.

Unbeknownst to me there is one dog that keeps catching my wife's eye as she searches the internet, a certain Mr Spencer who is available through a small West Country based rescue called Starfish. She eventually shows me his profile and straight away I can see why she has been drawn to him as he has a beautifully friendly look about him. When Chriss makes enquiries she's told that there is another family interested who if they pass a home check will be taking the dog. A home check is pretty much an interview to confirm your eligibility to own the dog where a responsible person visits your house to make sure you're suitable for each other. However after my wife has discussed our background to the lady running the rescue she says she has a really good feeling about us and would prefer us to become Mr Spencer's new owners. He's already been let down by one family who returned him saying he was too boisterous for their small children so she's incredibly keen for him to go to the right home this time.

A few days later there's a knock at the door, it's time for us to be vetted to see if we're suitable to be doggy parents. After a look round the house including a check of the outdoor space we face a number of questions such as how we intend to exercise the dog, provide day care and the like. Once the home check has been completed the wheels of motion move rapidly to finalise the adoption of Mr Spencer who is currently being fostered in south Wales by Julie Wright, a volunteer for Starfish.

At the very beginning of January 2014 my wife and I are sat in a coffee shop at a motorway services just north of Birmingham waiting to collect the newest member of our family. The weather is typically wintry, it's cold, grey, damp and miserable. We've arranged with

Julie to meet half way which is about a three hour drive for both of us. We meet her in a surreptitiously quiet corner of the carpark as though we're about to conduct a drug deal instead of collecting a dog. After having Jack we are used to big dogs but when Spencer jumps out of the boot then greets us by standing on his hind legs and placing his front paws on my shoulders we are both taken aback somewhat by his size. No wonder Julie affectionately calls him 'my little pony'. We let him stretch his legs for ten minutes or so before we say our goodbyes, poor Julie is quite emotional as she has grown rather attached to him over the last few weeks. On the long journey home Spencer just rests his head over the back seats and stares at us, he must be wondering what the fuck is going on. That evening when we put him to bed we are prepared for a sleepless night but to his credit after a couple of minutes of whining he settles down and we don't hear a peep from him until the morning.

We discover that Spencer was found by himself at only a few months old wandering the streets of Mazarron in Spain by the remarkable Gill Minnican who runs Starfish Rescue whilst she was at her holiday home and subsequently placed him in the care of its Spanish affiliate Little Starfish so he could be assessed and rehomed. Given that dogs especially sighthounds have such large litters I've often wondered what happened to Spencer's siblings, I think he was probably dumped along with the rest of them as puppies often are in Spain but what happened to the others. I'd like to know but at the same time maybe it's best not knowing after some of the stories I've heard.

We find out that Spencer is most likely a cross breed of Galgo Espanol and Podenco neither of which we have ever heard of which prompts us to search the internet for answers. Unfortunately what we learn is that these animals are subjected to horrendous and despicable treatment by their owners the *Galgueros*.

Galgo Espanol or Spanish greyhound are a very old breed of sighthound and it is believed that the English greyhound is a descendant of them with the two being cross bred during the 1900s to produce faster more powerful hounds. References to the Galgo have been found dating back to Roman times with them originally being considered a dog of nobility being kept mostly by the aristocracy during the Middle Ages. In fact it seems tragically ironic given how Galgos are persecuted today being considered no more than 'trash dogs' that they were held in such high esteem with laws made to prevent the killing and theft of them, even being bequeathed in wills demonstrating how valuable they were to their owners.

Although very similar in appearance there are distinct differences between a Galgo and a domestic greyhound. Whilst greyhounds are the Usain Bolt of the dog world, Galgos are more of an Ed Moses type possessing more stamina and endurance. I've seen Spencer run with a pure grey and whilst he wasn't quite as fast he was still ready to run when the grey was trying to catch its second wind. Other physical differences are that Galgos tend to be of a slightly smaller, lighter build with a less deep chest and with long streamlined heads making the ears appear larger. Also Galgos unlike greys can be found with a rough coat and in a variety of colours, Spencer being a rough coated red (rojo) fawn.

Despite the few physical differences both breeds have very similar temperaments being placid, docile and extremely lazy. It's a common misconception that they need lots of exercise, the number of times I've been stopped and asked 'he must take some walking' when actually they are more than happy to sleep most of the day. Spencer regularly spends several hours of an evening on his sofa without moving. They are gentle, tolerant creatures good with other dogs and people but can be reserved and somewhat aloof so if you're looking for a very affectionate animal they're probably not the best choice. However if you want a dog that is low maintenance, requires little exercise and can be left to its own devices for long periods a greyhound will suit you perfectly. Another positive for me is that they are very quiet dogs rarely barking at all.

The Galgo is a hunting dog used mainly for hare coursing on the plains of Spain which has encouraged the growth of competitions to find the galguero with the best specimen of the breed. As a result this has contributed to massive overbreeding to produce the perfect hunting dog with the rest being discarded in extremely heinous and inhumane ways. Galgos are treated like a commodity with puppies being abandoned on the streets much like Spencer was with the ones that make the grade fairing no better. The dogs are often kept in terrible conditions, emaciated, neglected and forcibly trained usually by being tied to the back of a car that is then driven at speed for miles. Injuries and unhealthy dogs go untreated with only the fittest surviving. Even the ones that fulfil their potential are on borrowed time as generally by the age of three the galgueros consider them to be too old for the hunt. It is estimated that approximately fifty thousand Galgos are abandoned or *disposed* of at the end of every hunting season. A particularly appalling pastime used by the galguero is what's known colloquially as 'the piano dance' where the dog is hung from a tree with the hind legs just barely touching the floor as it slowly strangles to death. It's not uncommon for dogs to be remorselessly shot, blinded and limbs broken then left to a slow agonising death. Others are just dumped becoming feral existing by scavenging hence the moniker trash dogs, whilst their luck holds out as the majority of the Spanish public turn a blind eye to this massive problem.

One of our social media friends who is a supporter of the Challenge adopted a Galgo bitch from Spain which had been viciously attacked by her owner who'd taken a claw hammer to her skull. How the poor animal survived let alone made a full recovery without any lasting damage is a sheer miracle the only reminder of the trauma being the obvious scar on her forehead.

For many, many years this has been Spain's dirty secret but fortunately the plight of the Galgo is being highlighted in the mainstream media gaining massive support across the globe. Numerous rescues have been created mainly by expats to provide assistance but struggle against the tide of the overwhelming numbers that need help whilst the galgueros continue their gruesome outdated traditions.

It doesn't take long to fall completely head over heels in love with Spencer, I doubt he'd win Best Mongrel at Crufts but he's by far the best in my show, mainly because he's such a handsome dog with such a lovely temperament, he really is a gentle giant. He's a happy boy who loves meeting people and fantastic with other dogs although bigger fluffier dogs than himself do tend to put the wind up him. The only things he doesn't like are thunderstorms and fireworks as well as having a strange phobia of balloons. He likes to sit in front of the mirrors in the bedroom checking himself out, mind you if I was that good looking I'd be doing the same. He has these beautiful rows of black dots on the end of his nose, his amber eyes are ringed by black guyliner with the cutest ginger eyelashes and a set of huge pearly white gnashers any big cat would be proud of. His rough coat is known as red fawn in the business but that's ginger to a layman like myself, with a snowy white undercarriage and a lion's mane covering his thick muscular neck. The back of his hind legs which look like they have been chiselled from stone are covered in fluffy white almost down like fur. There's no denying he's a greyhound, he runs like the wind but he's happiest lazing the day away roaching, this is where they lie on their back, front legs in the air hind legs spread-eagled. Spencer is also totally food obsessed, how he'd have managed living on the streets fending for himself I really do not know. I swear he wears a watch, it has four settings; dinnertime, teatime, sofa time and bedtime.

Being inexperienced sighthound owners soon brings about a few surprises, mostly whilst out on walks. With Jack we could let him off the lead almost anywhere satisfied that he wouldn't wander far but the first time we let Spencer loose that's it he's off like a shot. And he has zero recall. He's chased cats across busy main roads, chased the trams on the prom crossing the tracks into the road and almost ended up in Fleetwood on several occasions chasing seagulls on the beach. And let me tell you, you do not want to have to give chase after a dog that can achieve speeds well in excess of thirty miles per hour. There's only going to be one winner in that race. I suppose he's already used a few of his nine lives and I'm sorry to say that is completely our fault but fortunately no harm has been done. We've learnt from our mistakes and we have also learnt to recognise the triggers to the point where he is now only ever let off the lead at the beach if there's the minimal of distractions.

Nevertheless I could probably write a complete chapter of superlatives about what a fantastic dog Spencer is however it would be verbose of me to wax lyrical about how amazing he is, but honestly we couldn't have hoped for a better dog and let me assure you he had huge boots to fill after our Jack.

And then came Olive. Crazy little Olive.

When we decided to get a companion for Spencer it was a foregone conclusion that we wanted to offer a home to another rescued Spanish hunting dog given what we had learned.

Olive was rescued at only a few weeks old along with her five siblings in Jalon, Spain by the wonderful Jayne Webb, an expat who set up Jalon Valley A.R.C. along with Sally Mason and has lived in the valley for over fifteen years. Unfortunately the only male puppy of the litter perished, whilst Jayne kept two siblings Olive and her two other sisters were all rehomed in the UK. Olives mother a Podenco was a street dog who had been seen scavenging in Jalon and had quite obviously not long since given birth. For the safety of her litter she had hidden them in the deep roots of an old carob tree on the hillside above the town which is where Jayne was finally able to track her down bringing about the rescue of the pups. Tassia as she is now called remained a feral street dog for several more months until she was finally rescued and rehomed along with one of Olives sisters in North Yorkshire to the lovely Kate and Eric Howey who have since emigrated to Spain to do their bit for hunting dogs so moved were they by the plight of the Podenco.

It is Jaynes belief that the puppies were fathered by two different males, I wasn't aware this was possible but apparently so, if a dogs semen remains viable in the bitches uterus whilst she produces her eggs therefore there is the potential for multiple fathers. Nobody knows what breed Olives father is but we do know her mother is a Podenco.

Podenco is a generic term which translated from Spanish means hound. There are numerous kinds of Podenco depending usually on geographical origin such as Podenco Canario, Andalusian hound, Podenco Ibicenco and Portugese Podengo to name a few. Podencos are sight hounds with excellent hearing and a keen sense of smell being used primarily for hunting rabbits and vermin and are often used alongside Galgos. They are generally a medium sized strong, muscular and sturdy dog but size can depend on origin some being as big as a Galgo or conversely terrier sized tending to be white, chocolate and fawn in colour possessing both rough and smooth coats with a long face and extremely large pointed ears. Other remarkably unusual features of the breed are that their nose, nails and skin tend to be a pinkish colour which is known to 'blush' depending on the mood of the animal as well as having strikingly amber coloured eyes.

The Podenco is just as persecuted as the Galgo, in some cases even more so and has become known as 'the great forgotten' due to the lack of publicity regarding the abusive treatment they endure. They are often kept in squalid dark sheds or even underground caves which can cause them to go blind, usually chained up for long periods and in such large packs that they can barely move whilst being forced to *live* in their own faeces and urine. The galgueros believe they hunt better when hungry so just like the Galgo they are rarely fed becoming extremely emaciated causing health problems none of which receive medical treatment. Despite being loyal and affectionate they are starved of any human contact which can make them become withdrawn, skittish and petrified of human beings.

In a tragic twist of fate Podencos along with Galgos and other hunting dogs are viewed as worthless and very rarely wanted as pets by the Spanish resulting in huge numbers of them ending up in *perreras,* Spanish for dog pound but also colloquially known as *kill stations* where the Podencos are generally amongst the first dogs to be euthanized. This is all the more tragic considering that Podencos actually make such wonderful pets if only given the chance.

My wife returns to the internet but this time with more focused purpose as we now know exactly what we are looking for. After a couple of disappointing knockbacks we find little Olive who is currently being fostered through Kent Greyhound Rescue with one of their volunteers the marvellous Laura Cording. In an ironic twist of fate this time the home check is to be conducted by our next door neighbours daughter who has known us for many years, needless to say she signs us off without hesitation.

January 1st 2015

Olive is being fostered in Broadstairs, Kent where one of our closest friends comes from which seems like a good omen but is about as far away as you can be without speaking French. I've stayed at home to look after Spencer whilst my wife makes the long journey south to the prearranged rendezvous point somewhere on the M1 south of Birmingham. Unfortunately Olive is a very poor traveller by all account, I'm guessing she found the two day road trip from Spain rather traumatic, so my wife has taken reinforcements in the shape of her mother and her mother's friend Paula, who has since become our go to number one doggy day care provider, to help on the way home.

Around lunch time I get a call from my wife 'She's tiny!' she exclaims with a squeal.

The plan is that I'll take Spencer to the nearby playing fields where my wife will meet me with Olive so that they can be introduced on neutral ground rather than Spencer having his territory infiltrated by our new interloper.

When I see my wife's car enter the car park I make my way across the football pitch as she retrieves Olive from the boot and quite frankly I'm taken aback with shock. She really is tiny! She is so thin you can see every bone in her little body especially down her spine and round her hips. In the forthcoming weeks both my wife and I are stopped and reprimanded by fellow dog walkers suggesting that we should feed our dog. Olive is much less than half the size of Spencer who seems even bigger next to his new sister, after a cursory almost disinterested sniff Spencer carries on about the more pressing business of finding exactly the right spot to relieve himself. Olive is white with chocolate markings just like a little moo cow and in stark contrast to Spencer's rough coat hers is beautifully smooth like a velvet glove. She also possesses the large ears, hazel eyes with the pink nose, feet and belly that are common attributes of the Podenco breed.

Olive quickly makes herself at home and within no time it feels like we've never been without her. What she lacks in size she certainly makes up for in personality, she's very affectionate, cheeky, sassy, boisterous, mischievous and energetic not to mention incredibly cute and adorable. In fact that was her only saving grace when she was going through her chewing phase. As she reveals her bossy side Spencer takes on the role of the hen pecked husband, I feel sorry for him but it's his own fault for being such a big soft lump, I don't doubt that Jack would have put her right in her place. Despite being a right bossy boots she gets rather jealous when we show affection to Spencer. Jayne later reveals to us that Olive always was the leader of the pack which doesn't surprise us at all. If we visited a dog psychologist, yes there are such people, the diagnosis would be that Olive is as mad as a box of frogs. Olive soon melts our hearts and being very much a daddy's girl quickly becomes my 'little Princess'.

Despite being like chalk and cheese in terms of size and temperament the similarities between the sighthound breeds is very obvious. I doubt Spencer would have been of much use to Mr Galguero though as he is far too lazy unless he's catching bees in the garden yet Olive on the other hand is a ferociously tenacious and focused hunter. She's caught all kinds of animals from mice and rabbits to various species of bird and even hedgehogs. It's quite a sight to behold actually when she's in the zone as she performs these huge leaps into the air stamping into the ground in an attempt to unsettle and flush out her prey. I'm glad I'm not a mouse living on Blackpool prom.

The best thing we ever did was get a companion for Spencer though at times I doubt he'd agree but I think he does love Olive. She definitely loves him. He doesn't love her enough to share his sofa though, that is definitely not up for negotiation.

It strikes me as incredibly amusing now to think that in my previous life I was very scornful of and quick to mock those strange doggy people who treated their pets like surrogate children as I have become one of them. I have joined the pack and in all honesty it has enriched my life making me a better person.

Love is a four legged word.

A Saturday in Hell

'These bloodied and battered warriors struggle through the rain, the cold, the mud, on roads better suited to oxen cart than bicycles. But for the victor there is glory, immortality and a place in history amongst the giants of the road.'
John Tesh (CBS commentator)

December 2013
I'm sat at the computer, the Paris Roubaix Challenge website page is open in the browser and my right hand index finger hovers over the mouse ready to register to ride my favourite race and arguably the hardest of them all.

I hesitate.

A niggling seed of doubt has suddenly invaded my mind. I consider my options. Am I really ready not to mention brave enough to tackle 'the hell of the north'. The furthest I've ridden in one day for a very long time is about a hundred kilometres and that was several years ago. I consider signing up for the 145km route but that is still the best part of ninety miles, including all that horrible pave. I immediately dismiss the shorter route, I'm not going to travel all the way to northern France for a forty odd mile bike ride. Besides if I'm going to attempt it I'm determined to tackle the full distance but that seed of doubt has suddenly grown into a huge old oak tree of doubt.

I'm not afraid to admit it but I chicken out.

There and then I make a pact with myself that instead of riding the Challenge in 2014 I will spend all next year training for it and be ready to take on the pave in 2015.

Sunday 31st August 2014
I'm sat in the car in Wythenshawe park watching other riders preparing their bikes and themselves to ride the Manchester100 sportive. It's grey and miserable with incessant drizzle, typical Manchester weather. Little wonder then that Morrissey wrote the lyrics 'it's Manchester, it's gruesome'. Brilliant, I love British

summertime. And I love getting wet on the bike even less. I've upheld my side of the pact with some pretty serious training over the last few months and decided several weeks ago that I needed to test myself in a long distance sportive. In my search for a suitable event I've discovered that the Manchester100 is a relatively flat and fast scenic course looping through Cheshire where a fairly strong rider can post a good time. There's a choice of two distances, 100 miles or 100 kilometres. We've opted for the century, I say we, as I've managed to rope in my best cycling buddy Alan. He's also recruited a work colleague, Mark whom I've never met, who tells us as we gripe about the weather that he's never ridden further than thirty miles in a single day before. Really?! My mood darkens even further to match the weather outside. With all the enthusiasm I can manage to muster I leave the warm, dry comfort of the car and prepare to get wet.

The organisers are releasing groups of twenty riders at one minute intervals and by 8am we are rolling away from the Start banner heading south for the Cheshire plains. The first hour or so is pretty damp but soon dries out and turns into a half decent day. The route was described on the website as being scenic and I have to agree rural Cheshire is a very nice part of the world, and despite a few cheeky undulations is pleasantly flat. The event has attracted numerous participants which provide us with the opportunity of there being plenty of groups on the road to ride with which we can use to get towed along and by the time we take a comfort break after about three hours we have made good progress having covered almost half the distance.

Strangely it takes a while to get the legs going again after our rest stop then after about seventy miles as we negotiate a couple of roundabouts I notice my two companions are a good few bike lengths back down the road. I ease up on the pedals to allow them to rejoin me and within a minute or so Alan draws alongside but without Mark.

'Where's Mark?' I enquire. Alan tells me that he's feeling it a bit and didn't want to hold us back.

We ride along in silence for a few miles before stopping for another comfort break. As we are about to get going again Mark rolls to a stop beside us. We give him a minute to sort himself out then set off at speed back towards Wythenshawe. However it doesn't take long to drop Mark but this time we don't ease up and carry on setting a pretty fast pace. The only downside of the route is that it's pretty built up as we near Wythenshawe and there seems to be a distinct lack of courteous road users in this area.

As we enter the park and make the final approach to a very busy finish area I offer Alan my hand. He shakes it 'Well done pal' he says. About ten minutes later we clap Mark over the line.

According to my Strava app I've ridden 102.6 miles in 5 hours 53 minutes.

So now I know I'm ready for 'the hell of the north'.

Earlier in the year I'd been granted a transfer at work and in the general getting to know my new colleagues the topic of cycling had come up, it was mentioned in conversation that a guy named Murph had ridden that years Paris Roubaix. I sought out this warrior of the road eager to glean any tips and knowledge from him that I could. It turns out he'd paid several hundred pounds for a fully organised and supported trip run by a company called Sporting Tours which I had heard of. His enthusiasm for the race and the pave was instantly evident and he admitted unashamedly that before the race he'd bought any and all equipment that bore the names *Roubaix* or *pave* on it from tyres to water bottle cages.

'So what time did you manage?' I ask getting straight to the point.

His response of 'Six and a half hours' impresses me, I'd been told that he was a very strong rider who loved a few beers as much as he did cycling. Perfect, a man after my own heart.

He goes on to tell me that he's organising a trip to next years' race and I'm more than welcome to join them. I mention how it's always been the one race I'd like to do but I omit telling him about bottling out of the event this year.

Apparently after he'd returned from northern France he'd been regaling members of the triathlon club in the pub with tales of the pave who suggested if it was that good he should put a trip together.

And that's how I find myself at 5am on a Friday morning on the station yard boarding a minibus bound for Dover and a boat to northern France.

In the run up to our departure word seems to have got round the station about our trip so much so I've been asked the same question that many times I now have a stock answer like some kind of media spokesperson. What they want to know is 'What time are you going to do?' what I tell them and what I think are two different things. I tell them I'm hoping to complete the distance in less than seven hours but the real truth is I'll be happy just to finish.

I have five travelling companions, Murph obviously it's his trip and Moose I know but the other three lads I've never met before. The other three are Jack, Rainford and Nozza, with the exception of Jack all of them are veterans of many Ironman triathlons although Jack has apparently done a lot of cycling with Rainford who is supposedly a strong rider whilst Murph has already finished a 'hell of the North'. I've never ridden with any of them so this could be interesting to say the least.

The motorway journey south is refreshingly uneventful but we arrive in Dover having just missed a ferry which unfortunately means we have a two hour wait for the next one. The implications of this are felt later on in the day when we hit rush hour traffic around Lille and by the time we arrive at the velodrome in Roubaix to collect our registration documents it's almost 6pm. Quick as a flash before any of us can join him Murph has disappeared in search of the registrations booth. I've got to see the velodrome though so Jack and I go for a quick wander, and there she is in all her crumbling glory where hopefully tomorrow I will ride those boards after a day in hell. We have just enough time to take the obligatory picture in front of the huge cobblestone plinth at the entrance to the velodrome, donated by Les Amis de Paris Roubaix on the races 100th anniversary before Murph returns looking stressed. More importantly he's also empty handed. Apparently registration closed at 6pm so we must have missed it by a matter of minutes. We head away from Roubaix feeling somewhat deflated when Murphs mobile phone starts ringing. After a brief exchange he ends the call and performs a U turn. The person calling him is from Registrations and has been waiting especially for us to turn up.

Murph eventually returns with six white A5 sized sealed envelopes. He hands one to each of us, there's a sticker with my

name and the number 8 on it in small black type. Contained in the envelope is:-
2 x small zip ties, a A4 sized route map, a pocket sized route card, a long thin red sticker with the details of all secteurs of pave to be placed on the bikes top tube, a ticket for the coach to Busigny and a A6 black, white and red card with my race number on it to be attached to the handlebars using the aforementioned zip ties. On the back is a plastic timing chip which will monitor my progress along the route.

By the time we've negotiated all the one way systems around Lille centre and eventually located our hotel it is well after 7pm so we check in, dump the bags and go out for something to eat. Friday night must be party night in Lille as all the bars and restaurants are doing a roaring trade and there are a lot of people milling about. The hotel Murph has chosen, because it has a large public bar with an extensive menu of local beers, is a busy place and when we return ready to head to bed the joint is absolutely bouncing with revellers in various states of inebriation. Unfortunately I'm a very light sleeper so despite being two floors up and wearing ear plugs the noise from the bar is still very noticeable. Also my room is at the front of the hotel so all the passing traffic rattling over the cobbles adds to my misery. It is well after midnight before it starts to quieten down and I'm going to be up in a couple of hours to tackle the hardest ride of my life, hardly the ideal preparation.

Fanfuckingtastic!

Saturday 11th April 2015

It feels like I've been asleep for minutes when Nozza shakes me awake.

'C'mon mate it's time to get ready, I'll see you downstairs.' He says.

With bleary eyes I check my mobile, its 4am yet surprisingly I don't actually feel *that* tired. The night before I've organised my gear so within minutes I'm ready to go and head downstairs to the now eerily quiet dark bar. The others are already waiting for me and after a cursory 'Morning' we step out into the cold blackness. We manage to park virtually opposite the entrance to the velodrome and set about last minute checks of both our bikes and ourselves. I squeeze my tyres and decide to let out a couple of psi, just for luck. Hugging the right hand side of the road sit a convoy of black coaches with bike carriers hitched to the rear. After a few minutes of searching we find the coach we've been allocated to and join the queue of other riders waiting to load their bikes. Once aboard I find a seat by myself near the toilet in case I need a nervous piss.

I have to congratulate the organisers for handling so efficiently the logistics of ferrying well over a thousand riders and their bikes the ninety minute journey from Roubaix down to the start in Busigny.

By the time we arrive it's starting to get light which reveals a very grey, overcast sky. One of the more printable nicknames my wife has for me is 'weather boy' because I'm obsessed with checking it whilst planning my training rides. I've been studying the weather for today for the previous week and while it has been fine and dry all week the forecast for today is cloudy with showers. Fabulous. As we disembark we feel the drizzle hit us, Murph responds to my moaning about the weather,

'Well you want the full experience don't you Ritch!' and throws me a knowing wink.

We follow the marshal's directions to the Start and are greeted by the boom boom of euro pop. It's an open start which means there's no fanfare you just turn up and go. As we *officially* get under way the drizzle has become full blown rain, this could get tasty, very tasty indeed.

In the weeks and even months prior to embarking on this trip I've been doing as much research as possible about the race in the hope of picking up some tips to make my journey over the cobbles easier. The recurrent theme seems to be about tyres and pressures, most advice being to use a wider treaded tyre of at least 27mm with reduced pressures of as low as 5 bar (73psi) whereas normally I would probably use a 23mm slick tyre running 8 bar. The reason for this is to increase grip and the amount of rubber on the road but most importantly to reduce the risk of punctures on the pave. It seems your hands take a battering from gripping the bars on the uneven surfaces so many pros not only use a double layer of handlebar tape but also tape their hands in preparation for combat. Murph had already told me of his experience last year when hitting the first secteurs of pave of bidons flying all over the place.

I'd considered buying the tyres Murph recommended but my frugal mind decided that I couldn't justify spending nearly a hundred quid on a pair of tyres that I'm only going to use just once so in my infinite wisdom I decide to make do with the Bontrager Race 25mm slick tyres I already have on my bike. I've opted for pressures of almost 7 bar as any less just doesn't feel right to ride on. Rooting about in the garage one day I come across what I can only describe as a very thin yet supple kind of pipe lagging polystyrene which has the ideal diameter to fit my handlebars. I cut it down to size and wrap it in place with black electrical tape, job done. I also wrap my bidons with a couple of layers electrical tape about halfway up, hopefully this will provide enough resistance to stop them from bouncing out of their cages. On the coach down to Busigny I carefully wrap my hands with microporous tape then put on an old yet comfortable pair of full finger gloves. If lady luck is on my side I should smash this.

Almost the first ten miles are on fairly smooth tarmac with the first secteur, rated three stars and 2.2km long coming at Troisvilles a Inchy. Apparently the best way to ride the pave is to ride on the crown down the centre of the road and go as hard as possible to keep the speed up which reduces the vibration and impact from the irregularity of the cobbles. It's best to stay relaxed without gripping the handlebars too tightly and you will also see the pros riding in the gutter on both sides of the road in search of a smoother passage. Now this is attainable if you're a hard as nails beyond super fit pro but if like me you're a mere mortal then being able to ride 27 interval sprints, some as long as two and a half miles, in over a hundred miles well Chapeau to you. Something I hadn't realised whilst studying the route is that once the pave starts at Troisvilles there is very little respite between secteurs until you reach the outskirts of Roubaix which means you have only a limited amount of time to recover from the physical effort and punishment the pave dishes out on each secteur.

Another aspect of the Challenge which I hadn't been expecting and as a purist really doesn't sit very well with me is the number of participants riding mountain bikes. In my opinion the organisers should prevent people from taking part on them because it detracts from the whole ethos of the race. Don't get me wrong I have absolutely nothing against mountain bikes per se but the reason why Paris Roubaix is so revered is because it's about tackling an extremely tough course on a traditional road bike with only minor adaptations which in reality is completely unsuitable for the terrain. I mean you wouldn't turn up to a speedway race on a motocross bike would you. During the course of the day I found them to be nothing more than a bloody nuisance and challenge each and every one of them to give it a go as I believe it should be ridden.

As we approach the very first secteur of pave the pace of the group increases noticeably and we naturally string out to form a single file of riders. I'm sure I hear somebody shout 'Here we go lads!' but I can't be certain as the immediate future is about to become very blurred. At the start of every secteur there is a banner overhead and a sign which tells you the name, star rating, distance and number of secteur. I have just enough time to read the number 27 and that it is rated three stars before all hell breaks loose.

Jesus fucking Christ!

The sensation of hitting those cobbles is like being handed a pneumatic jackhammer on full speed setting. Suddenly the horizon becomes a complete blur as my eyes are shaken in their sockets, I hold onto the bars with a vice like grip and I'm positive if I could see my knuckles they would be bone white. Grown men are screaming, yes actually screaming. Others are cursing loudly, some are laughing but it's not a happy, joyous laugh it's a scared and maniacal laugh like Jack Nicholson in The Shining. Bidons and other personal items are flying all over the place as riders jockey for position desperate to find the smoothest possible line. The pace has slowed considerably, well mine certainly has as I try to focus just ahead of my bouncing front wheel, yet I'm breathing hard and it feels like my heartrate has gone through the roof. This first secteur is 2.2km long so even at a pace as slow as mine the battering *only* lasts just over five minutes, however it feels like it's never going to end. In all the excitement I hadn't even noticed that it had stopped raining.

Did I really *want* to do this? What I soon come to realise is that on the pave you are totally alone and there is nowhere to hide, it's just you and your machine against the cobbles. All the tips I'd learnt and best intentions I had about how to ride the pave go completely out the window as I hang on for dear life, trying my damnedest not to fall off or even worse take somebody else out. To my absolute relief the banner signalling the end of the secteur hovers into view and I feel like a cork being pulled from a bottle as I throw myself onto the tarmac. Ah, smooth asphalt never felt so good.

We soon regroup and looking around I see my riding companions are still with me, the sense of shock at what we have just experienced is almost palpable. A rider in a bright red and yellow jersey emblazoned with '*Stockport Clarion*' draws alongside and asks us which station we're from, you can't fail to notice my cycling comrades all dressed in their Fire & Rescue Service emblazoned lycra. He tells us 'I'm from Red watch, King Street anyway have a good un lads' then powers away from us, small world isn't it. We also have an interloper in our group, a bloke named Alex from London has joined us and as we ride the conversation is about what else, cycling of course.

Alex reveals how this is his third time taking on the Challenge and how only last Saturday he completed the Ronde van Vlaanderen Cyclo for the second time. 'Wow, that's awesome!' I say unable to conceal the jealousy in my voice. He goes on to tell me how the pave in Flanders is much smoother, not so haphazard and better maintained which makes it a lot easier to ride. He'll watch the race tomorrow then be back home two hours later and be able to have a couple of beers before work on Monday, unlike the seven hour journey home we have to look forward to, which makes it ideal to hop over for a weekend of cycling and Belgian beer. I ask him if he always rides alone to which he responds that this year he has been after his riding partner crashed on a secteur of pave and broke his femur during last years' Challenge. Jesus, I'm nervous enough without hearing stories like that! Suddenly as if on cue from behind us comes that dreadful metallic clang as someone takes a fall, instinctively we all crane our necks round like a mob of meerkats to look in macabre fascination just glad it isn't us. Nobody stops to offer assistance. Only a few hundred metres further on we come to a T junction where we are directed to turn right, on the opposite pavement a rider stands clutching his elbow in the obvious pose of someone who's broken a collarbone.

Soon enough the chatter in the group abates and there's an increased sense of nervousness as we approach the next secteur. I decide to get on Alex's wheel and try to follow him, if he's ridden this and De Ronde so many times he probably has a better idea of what he's doing than I do. After a few hundred metres he begins to pull away from me and I find myself behind Rainford, in the near distance I can see we are rapidly catching a much slower rider who seems intent on keeping his line on the crown. Judging from Rainfords body language it looks like he has the same idea as me, in my head I say to myself 'I'm having this' and with a few hard turns of the pedals move round Rainford on his right cutting him up just as he's about to pass the rider ahead. As I power pass both riders all I hear is Rainford shouting after me 'You fucking wanker!' whether or not he knew it was me at the time I don't know as I'm wearing fairly nondescript cycling gear but we have a right laugh about it over a few beers later that night.

The next few secteurs are literally a blur, however I seem to have gained a bit more confidence and settled my nerves somewhat. I'm still riding in the company of Alex, even though he distances me on the pave I'm able to catch him up once back on the tarmac or maybe he just lets me get back on. I spot some of my travelling companions in the group but can't be certain as to the whereabouts of all of them. Just as I'm getting into a really nice rhythm the first 'Feed Zone' appears and everyone pulls over, why are we stopping now for fucks sake we've not even been riding two hours yet! As we refill our bidons and grab some food someone asks 'Where's Nozza?' then right on cue we see him fly past like he's got the devil himself chasing him, we shout after him but to no avail. It'll be several hours before I see my roommate again.

Up until now the weather has held and despite the earlier rain the pave remains relatively dry. As we approach secteur 19 at Haveluy a Wallers rated 4 stars at two and a half kilometres in length I again take up a position behind Alex with another rider in front of him.

What we don't notice until it's too late is that the start of this secteur is covered in a film of black greasy mud, the rider in front panics losing his front wheel and in a split second goes down. Alex has no time to react going straight into the back of the prone rider sending him flying sideways, somehow more by luck than design I manage to swerve avoiding both of them and fortunately stay upright. I ask the eternally inane question 'Are you ok?' The other rider is already up but Alex flounders in the mud like a fish out of water in the middle of the road. Riders are trying to get past so I help him up and get us to the side of the road. He's complaining about his wrist but after a quick check both he and his bike seem pretty much alright. We carry on somewhat gingerly at first but soon regain our momentum with the rest of the secteur passing uneventfully. In all the excitement I seem to have become separated from the others.

There are a handful of smooth kilometres on the approach to the mining town of Arenberg, the numerous camper vans of travelling fans and the colliery pithead winding gear standing guard at the entrance to the forest are obvious landmarks that the most infamous secteur of pave is on the horizon. Alex starts looking down at his rear wheel, I know what he's about to say.

'I think I've got a flat' he remarks. We pull over and sure enough the rear tyre is very soft, I ask him if he wants me to wait and help but he tells me to crack on. We shake hands wishing each other good luck.

I never see him again.

Despite having ridden nine secteurs over some incredibly tough terrain there is nothing that can prepare you for the Arenberg, the pave here is absolutely brutal. On the approach to the secteur there is a barrier across the road which riders are required to negotiate, this is just as well given that the secteur starts off slightly downhill. Tomorrow the barrier will be raised for the pros who will hit this secteur at absolutely crazy speeds in excess of 30mph all fighting for a position at the head of the peloton!

I round the barrier and enter *Hell*.

The bike bounces almost uncontrollably beneath me as I search in vain for the smoothest line. There is no conceivable crown or gutter as you might find in the other secteurs with the pave being wet, muddy and incredibly slippery. Huge gaps between the stones seek to devour your wheel, some with sharp edges lying in wait to slice your tyres or even worse your skin should you fall here. On the right is a footpath which usually has barriers in place for the race to keep the fans safe but the organisers have yet to fully complete the job. Riders are diving for the safety of this footpath, if you can't beat them join them I say. The relief however is short lived as about two hundred metres further on we are cruelly forced back onto the pave. I take up a position on the extreme right, next to the barriers as there is a thin strip of grass encroaching onto the pave making progress slightly easier. My slow pace on the other secteurs now feels snail like yet, with the exception of the odd brave hero I actually seem to be holding my own. A quick daring glance up reveals the end is almost in sight, I really can't believe I've almost managed to survive the Arenberg. As I cross the timing strip an audible beep signals the end of the hardest and scariest mile and a half of cycling I've ever ridden in my life. I let out a huge sigh of relief.

There is one more secteur before the next 'Feed Zone' which passes unremarkably and as I pull in to refresh my bidons I bump into Moose, Jack and Rainford just as they are about to leave and they ask me if I want them to wait but I'm happier riding alone to be honest so I gratefully decline. Just before they set off Moose says 'Guess which soft wanker rode half of the Arenberg on the footpath?' before I can respond a huge smile crosses his face and he points at Rainford, both he and Jack burst out laughing like a pair of naughty schoolboys. I decide it prudent not to let on about doing exactly the same as I watch them clip in and ride off. See you later, much later.

After a quick comfort break I'm on my way heading for another long, hard 4 star rated secteur at Hornaing a Wandignies. Riding in the left hand gutter trying to avoid the crocodile teeth of pave I can see why this secteur has been awarded such a high rating. Suddenly my front wheel dives forward into a pothole and there's a horribly disconcerting bang as the tyre punctures instantly. There are two kinds of puncture, one is a penetration puncture where a foreign object such as a fragment of glass pierces through the tyre or the second, which I have just suffered is an impact puncture where the inner tube is pinched against the rim after being compressed against a sharp edge such as a pothole.

During my many years of cycling I've suffered my fair share of punctures and as a result I'm rather adept at changing an inner tube. Without panicking I dismount and move onto the grass verge out of the way of the other competitors. Within a couple of minutes I have the new tube in and begin inflating the tyre, all the while riders are rattling past me ten to the dozen which makes me feel rather isolated like I'm being left behind. I carefully pack away my repair kit in my pocket as the last thing I need is for it to bounce out whilst crossing the pave as every secteur I cross I see all manner of personal belongings that have been lost. At the very next two star rated secteur of Warlaing a Brillon I suffer yet another impact puncture, in hindsight I think the tyre was underinflated. No drama.

The next secteur is at Tilloy a Sars-et-Rosiares and is rated four stars. About halfway across I hit a particularly sharp egded cobblestone suffering my third puncture in a row, now I *do* start to panic. I'd started the race with four spare inner tubes which means I now only have one left with a dozen secteurs of pave still to negotiate including the infamously difficult five star secteurs of Mons-en-Pevele and Carrefour de l'Arbre. I recall several secteurs back seeing an inner tube which had made its bid for freedom from somebody's pocket, I rue not stopping to pick it up. Having despondently fixed the puncture I carry on across the pave on foot, head down, crestfallen. After a couple of hundred metres I'm aware that walking is going to take me all fucking day so I reluctantly remount my bike throwing caution to the wind.

Much of the route of Paris Roubaix criss crosses the area that was known as 'no man's land' during the First World War, so riders are never far away from the historical significance of the roads they're traversing. This has particular sentimental meaning for me as my maternal Great Grandfather Arthur Hamilton and his brother in law Andrew Lee were both killed in action here. Due to the incessant shelling and poor weather the Western front became a muddy quagmire leading to many casualties being lost to the land who consequently have 'no known grave'. My Great Grandfather was one of these unfortunate souls, however his name along with sixty thousand others are recorded in perpetuity on the magnificent Menin Gate Memorial to the Missing in Ypres. His brother in law is buried in the immaculately kept Dozinghem Commonwealth War Graves Cemetery in West Vleteren on the outskirts of Ypres.

My nerves are absolutely frazzled and my mind is in complete disarray and it is now I attempt to invoke the spirit of my fallen relatives to help get me through this modern day version of hell. At one point I'm so concerned about not reaching the finish I even begin to consider leaving the officially marked route and finding my own way back to Roubaix so I don't have to cross any more of that fucking pave, the problem is I haven't got a clue where I am let alone which direction to head off in. Two years later in the 2017 edition of the professional race a rider from the UAE team called Andrea Guardini will do exactly that, abandoning the race and getting lost before being picked up by the police riding along the motorway heading back towards Roubaix. My previously slow pace is now down to a crawl as I carefully try to pick the least dangerous line across the pave, my tactic now being to try and make up time lost on the smooth tarmac sections. This new approach seems to be working as the next few secteurs even the horrendously difficult Mons-en-Pevele pass without incident albeit very slowly.

Slowly slowly catchy monkey.

As I approach the final five star rated secteur of Carrefour de l'Arbre it begins to rain again. 'Oh come on give me a fucking break for fucks sake' I scream. There are only two more secteurs both rated at two star to go after this so if I can just get through here I'm almost home and dry. There is a refreshingly smooth gutter so I make a beeline for it, however there are several deep potholes to be negotiated. Surprisingly there are riders going even slower than I am which frustratingly forces me onto the pave several times to pass them. Even more annoying though are the wankers on mountain bikes who come barrelling past on their big fat tyres and suspension frames oblivious to my suffering.

I can see the famous café up ahead in the distance as the wind blows horizontal stinging rain into my face, I grit my teeth tasting the dust off the pave and put my head down hoping for the torture to end soon. Despite the immense fatigue I actually feel like I'm riding quite well and start to believe that I just might reach the cathedral of cycling.

The last two secteurs seem impossibly easy after the physical and emotional trauma I've recently suffered creating a sense of relief so strong it almost brings a tear to my eye. I mentally thank Arthur and Andrew for their help. There's about five miles of gloriously smooth tarmac which will deliver me to the velodrome so even if I have a mechanical at this stage I could literally walk to the finish. It's very busy with weekend traffic as I negotiate the two lane boulevard into Roubaix so I take extra care as I don't want some idiot knocking me off when I'm so close. I make the right turn onto the Rue Alexander Fleming and sit up spinning the pedals, I want to saviour every last wheel turn of this titanic journey whilst avoiding the many potholes. It strikes me as rather ridiculous now how I seek the smoothest patch of road after the battering my bike and I have endured over the last seven hours. The final right turn takes me onto the boards of the velodrome itself, riders are sprinting past me taking a high line on the banking as if they're in the running to win the race whilst others are showboating to the line. I drop to the bottom of the track onto the blue painted inside lane as I round the very final bend and simply freewheel across the finish line without any fanfare. I'm completely exhausted not to mention being soaking wet, covered in sweat and the dirt of 'the hell of the north' yet there's an enormously relieved but proudly satisfied smile enveloping my entire face.

However, it's fair to say the pave *smashed* me!

Strava Data for Paris Roubaix Challenge 2015:-
Distance   104.2 miles
Moving Time   7 hours 18 minutes
Average Speed   14.3mph
Elevation gain   1781ft

Waiting with Alan for Le Tour- Col du Galibier July 2005

Murder on his mind, one extremely wet and pissed off gendarme- Luz Ardiden July 2003

Our wedding day- Blythe Hall 6th October 2012

Jack our big silver boy

Enjoying 15 minutes of fame on Countdown with my 'other woman' Rachel Riley

Baywatch with Mr Spencer

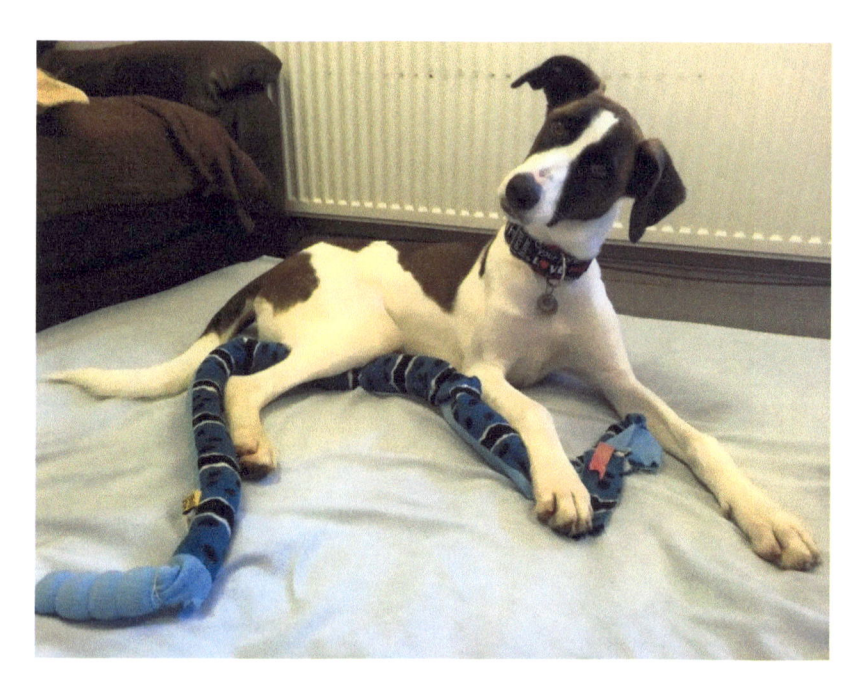

Daddy's Little Princess Olive

In Flanders Fields- paying respect to my relatives that were killed in World War 1

The iconic shower block awaiting the finishers at Paris Roubaix

Blowing out my arse on the Joux Plane during the 3rd Challenge-L'Etape 10th July 2016

Celebrating at the finish of each of the 3 Challenges

It's a family affair, my wife and I with Spencer and Olive

A Seed is Sown

'Whenever I see an adult on a bicycle, I do not despair for the human race.'
H G Wells (author)

Immediately after crossing the finish line I pull over to ring my wife Chriss.
'Hi darling it's me, I've just finished.' I announce matter of fact.
'Oh that's brilliant, how was it?' she asks
'It was fucking awful, never ever again!' I exclaim
She laughs 'Was it that bad?'
'No, it was worse than that. If I ever talk about doing anything like this again shoot me' I tell her. 'Well you've done it now, go and get yourself a beer' she replies cheerily.
We say our goodbyes then I slowly pedal round the other half of the velodrome towards the exit which is rather crowded with people, a young attractive French girl approaches and as she congratulates me gently places a finishers medal around my neck. As if by magic Nozza and Murph emerge from the gathered crowd, they must have seen me ride into the velodrome as we are parked immediately opposite the entrance. They seem in a hurry to get going, as they tell me everyone's waiting for me Nozza starts removing my race number from my handlebars he asks what size t-shirt I take.
'Medium' I answer sounding confused, 'Sure you're not a large?' he replies quizzically.
'No I'm definitely a medium, why?' I ask, 'You can exchange your race number for a shirt' he says and before I can respond disappears into the throng.
Murph ushers me back towards the van which I'm rather aggrieved about as I wanted to see the iconic shower block and buy a miniature version of the race winners cobblestone, but I'm too tired to protest and also aware that the others have probably been waiting for me for some time. As soon as we reach the van somebody else takes my bike from me so I climb aboard and laboriously change into

some dry clothes, all of my companions to a man look as wasted as I feel.

We drive back to the hotel in Lille reliving stories from our day in hell, I tell them about my misfortune with the punctures 'No wonder we were waiting for you for so fucking long!' shouts Murph. As soon as we enter the hotel I make a beeline for the bar and order a Leffe Blond my favourite Belgian beer which hardly touches the sides. I get myself another then head upstairs to get cleaned up. Later that evening in the bar Moose and Jack tell me how they had hatched a plan beforehand to make the ride as painful for Rainford as possible and said how at one point he was almost crying, they howled with laughter when I recounted my story of cutting him up on the pave.

Sunday 12th April 2015

After yet another very restless night, partly due to the noise from the bar and outside but also due to the nervous energy and adrenaline still coursing through my veins as I can't help but replay the events of the day in my mind, I make the effort to get up and believe me *it* is an effort. Everything hurts and when I say everything I mean everything. My hands are blistered, so much for taping them up, my arms and shoulders ache badly from gripping onto the bars and my perineum feels like it has taken a right kicking. Non cyclists always ask 'but doesn't it make your bum sore?' which is actually anatomically inaccurate however this morning it feels like I've been flogged. I don't know what being hit by a truck feels like but I'm guessing that it is pretty similar to how I now feel. I move about the room with all the vigour of an arthritic octogenarian making pitiful noises as I slowly get dressed. Today we are going to the Arenberg Forest to watch the pros stampede through, then dash back to the velodrome to catch the finale. The weather, of course is literally cracking the flags, bloody typical.

My number one fan and proud wife has updated her Facebook status with details of my 'heroic' exploits which has attracted several *Likes* and comments of congratulations. One such comment is from an old friend of hers, Lesley Morgan a fellow big doggie person involved in Weimaraner rescue, who asks us which charity her donation will be going to. Somewhat lamely we explain to her that I hadn't done the ride for charity, but that it was for my own selfish fulfilment and a case of ticking it off my bucket list. However that one simple question plants the seed of an idea in my head which over the next few months plays on my mind like an itch you just can't scratch.

Another thing that also happens relatively soon after finishing the 'hell of the north' is that I start to contemplate doing the race again. I know, I know I said never again but hey never say never again right. The human brain has a remarkable capacity for self-preservation which allows us to eventually forget painful and traumatic events, after all if it didn't women would only go through childbirth the once. This survival instinct enables us the ability to undertake unpleasant life events knowing the discomfort will only be relatively short lived. Don't get me wrong I'm no masochist and riding Roubaix left me hurting for several days afterwards but it gets under your skin and into your psyche. Unless you've ridden Paris Roubaix it's hard to explain the effect it has on you and without sounding pretentious I do feel like it has changed me and I begin to look at people differently comparing those who haven't ridden Roubaix to the experience I've had. But I suppose the same can be said of any significant life experience we go through.

The more I think about riding Paris Roubaix again the more I think about what Lesley said which makes me consider doing the race as a charity fundraiser. It appears that today *We* the British people have become a nation of givers and donators with people from all walks of life using all kinds of events to raise money for a variety of charities. The first such major charity fundraising event I can recall are the Live Aid concerts from 1985 organised by Sir Bob Geldof to help the people of Ethiopia affected by devastating famine. This seemed to inspire other initiatives such as Comic Relief many of which have now become annual events raising enormous amounts of money. Every time I turn on the television or look at social media nowadays it seems there is some worthy cause both at home and overseas appealing for monetary aid. Every tragic event or occurrence nowadays seems to within minutes have a *gofundme* page set up encouraging people to reach for their wallets.

So, in such a competitive environment how do I stand out from the crowd and inspire people to part with their hard earned cash and donate to my fundraiser?

Firstly the recipients of my fundraiser will be the animal rescues that saved my two dogs Olive and Spencer; Starfish Dog Rescue, Jalon Valley ARC and Kent Greyhound Rescue. As a nation of dog lovers I'm hoping this will persuade people to donate as I believe you'd be more inclined to give to a charity that affects and touches your own life.

Secondly from a personal point of view I'd be more inclined to donate to a cause if I deemed the event being used to fundraise was a worthy challenge. By that I mean I'd be unlikely to donate if the challenge was for example simply partaking in 'Dryanuary', that's not to undermine somebody's attempt it's just my personal opinion. Currently Sir Ranulph Fiennes is attempting the Global Reach Challenge in aid of Marie Curie, over twelve months he will be aiming to become the first person to cross both polar ice caps and climb the highest mountain on every continent known as the 'Seven Summits'. The Challenge has already raised in excess of two million pounds. Would it have generated as much interest if all he was doing was his local park run, I seriously doubt it.

Bearing this in mind I've decided to up the ante and include two other epic events as well as Paris Roubaix. This isn't to say I don't believe Paris Roubaix to be a worthy challenge, having ridden it quite the contrary but the bigger the challenge the bigger the rewards, at least that's what I'm hoping for. The chat with Alex during Roubaix about the Tour of Flanders has convinced me that I need to do this event and for the last couple of years I've been considering signing up for the L'Etape du Tour or quite simply a stage of the Tour de France. The details of the route for next years' L'Etape have been released and for a number reasons it looks very favourable. I have even thought of the name for the fundraiser, I'm going to call it ***'Ritch's 3 Tour Challenge'***.

I've always been quite an impulsive person however over the last few years I seem to have become less so, whether this is my wife's positive influence or I've simply grown up a bit I'm not sure. This is possibly why I don't actually broach the subject of the Challenge with Chriss until the very end of summer after a few months of contemplation and deliberation. That also explains why it's taken me so long to begin writing this book. She thinks it is a brilliant idea of course, and right away has some excellent ideas of her own to enhance the exposure of the Challenge such as creating our very own website amongst other things. As she's more computer savvy than myself I appoint her as head of the Challenge IT department as well as media officer and financial administrator, if there's anything else I've missed I apologise but I'm sure she'll put me straight. My role will quite simply be to put the miles in during training and complete the events as well as planning the logistics for the trips for each stage of the Challenge.

We begin by contacting each of chosen charities to outline our plans which are received with a mixture of surprise, gratitude and admiration. I imagine the hardest aspect of the Challenge for our charities will be waiting for the donations as we intend to open the Challenge in the New Year but the final event L'Etape isn't until the middle of July after which we will officially close the fundraiser. However this does provide us with the advantage of the opportunity to raise the profile of the Challenge for a longer more sustained period thereby hopefully maximising our fundraising potential.

My wife Chriss never ceases to amaze me, this is one of the many reasons why I married her, but the amount of work during her very limited free time that she puts into constructing our website and the other social media pages truly impresses me. She should be very proud of herself because I'm proud of her. Registrations for my chosen events don't open until the beginning of December so in the meantime I set about planning the logistics of each trip as well as making all the necessary bookings.

We're almost ready to go live.

Three is the Magic Number

'When it's hurting you, that's when you can make a difference.'
Eddy Merckx (the greatest cyclist of all time)

The three sportive events I have registered for my Challenge are:-

1st Challenge- Ronde Van Vlaanderen Cyclo

The first event of *Ritch's 3 Tour Challenge* will be the amateur version of one of the oldest, biggest and most prestigious one day races of the professional cycling calendar. The Ronde Van Vlaanderen or Tour of Flanders aka De Ronde is one of cycling's five monuments first being run in 1913 to promote circulation of the newspaper Sportwereld. It is one of the two major cobbled classics held on the first Sunday in April the week preceding Paris Roubaix and 2016 will be the one hundredth edition of Belgium's biggest race, estimated viewing figures for the previous years' race were two million people from a population of approximately twelve million. In a country where cycling is *the* number one sport De Ronde is the equivalent of the FA Cup and Champions League final all rolled into one so it should come as no surprise that the nation with the most victories is Belgium, taking an enormous sixty eight wins.

To date there has only been one British winner of De Ronde back in 1961 by Tom Simpson who is unfortunately more famous for collapsing during the 1967 Tour de France on the climb of Mont Ventoux. Major Tom as he was affectionately known amongst the peloton was one of the stars of the day and had a fearsome reputation for his ability to suffer on the bike. However on that fateful thirteenth stage he pushed himself too far and a combination of heat stroke and amphetamines, the drug of choice during that era, contributed to his death. A memorial to him now stands just short of the summit on the desolate, barren wind swept slopes where he fell that day never regaining consciousness.

If Bill Shankly the most famous manager of Liverpool football club had been a Flandrien no doubt he would have said 'Some people think De Ronde is a matter of life and death. I don't like that attitude. I can assure them it is much more serious than that.'

De Ronde is notorious for having a succession of short but very steep hills or bergs many of which are cobbled and very narrow, the most mythical being the poorly paved Koppenberg which despite being only 600 metres in length has pitches as steep as 22 percent where the cobbles are often incredibly wet and slippery. The final climbs of the race the Oude Kwaremont, the longest cobbled climb in Belgium and the very narrow and steep Paterberg are where the decisive moves of the race are usually made as they come so close to the finish. Since 1998 the race has started in the beautiful medieval city of Bruges then heads south along the flatlands of northern Belgium before encountering the bergs of western Flanders where all the action takes place leading to the final run in to the finish at Oudenaarde renowned for its gothic style town hall and market square but most importantly the *Centrum Ronde Van Vlaanderen* a cycling museum dedicated entirely to the race.

I'm happy to find out that 2016 will be the 25th edition of the Ronde Van Vlaanderen Cyclo as it almost seems to add more value to my first Challenge. Today it has become a huge event attracting some fifteen thousand riders from all over the world. When I register for the event there are three options to choose from, the complete 227 kilometre distance as raced by the professionals; a 129 kilometre course which tackles all the pave secteurs and cobbled bergs of the longer version or a shorter course covering just the final 71 kilometres but tackling the most iconic climbs on the route. Whilst researching the event I've discovered from online blogs that the first one hundred kilometres of the full race distance appear to be a tedious slog down a very busy highway before finally joining the medium distance route where it starts in Oudenaarde. The other drawback of the longer route is a logistical one as it starts over an hour's drive away in Bruges, although the organisers have laid on transport at an extra cost to return to Bruges but only at specific times. For these reasons my mind is made up on the medium route and also because I've decided to base myself an hour away from Oudenaarde in Ypres, so whilst I'm over there I can pay my respects to relatives killed during the Great War.

2nd Challenge- Paris Roubaix Challenge

The event that has inspired my Challenge will take place the weekend following the Ronde Van Vlaanderen Cyclo. This could work in one of two ways, it could be to my advantage in that hopefully by then I'll be in pretty good physical shape or adversely I'll be struggling from the after effects of the battering taken the weekend before.

Again I've opted for the full distance route of 172 kilometres including all twenty seven secteurs of pave which unfortunately involves the inconvenience of the ludicrously early morning call to be transported down to the start in Busigny.

3rd Challenge- L'Etape du Tour

The third and final event of my Challenge is L'Etape du Tour, in other words a stage of the Tour de France. L'Etape has been held every July since 1993 and covers the very same route of a mountain stage in either the Alps or Pyrenees. Unlike my other two Challenges for logistical reasons L'Etape takes place several days before the professional race but more importantly is held on closed roads which means all roads on the course are shut to the public and general traffic by the police. The event has become huge attracting a global participation of over fifteen thousand competitors including many ex professional cyclists and celebrities such as the only American winner of the Tour Greg Lemond and ex Formula 1 World Champion Alain Prost.

The very first edition of the Tour de France was held back in 1903 to promote the newspaper L'Auto being the brainchild of Henri Desgrange the editor in chief. His idealistic vision was to create a race so severe and physically demanding of the participants that only the strongest rider would make it to the finish. That first race was an instant success with the French public and has become so revered that it is now part of the culture of the nation. The mountains were first introduced to the race in 1910 in the Pyrenees when the roads were nothing but unmade tracks which seems incredible to me having ridden them that it was possible to traverse them on the bicycles of that age.

Of the three Grand Tours including the Giro d'Italia and Vuelta a Espana, the Tour de France is by far the oldest and most prestigious and has become a truly global spectacle. The three week multi stage race dominates the sporting calendar throughout the month of July following either a clockwise or anti clockwise journey around the country, usually but not always starting in France and finishing on the Champs Elysees in Paris hence the nickname 'La Grande Boucle' or large loop. The format for many years has involved a fairly flat terrain over the first week with stages suited to the sprinters which lead to the first set of mountain stages followed by a number of transitional stages taking the race into the last week and the final mountain stages where the battle for the maillot jaune (yellow jersey) is often played out before a transfer to Paris for the grandest of finales.

Despite the global popularity of Le Tour it was almost brought to a devastating end in 1998 following what has become known as the 'Festina Affair'. That year the race started in Irelands capital Dublin where Britain's very own and in my opinion vastly underrated Chris Boardman won the opening prologue time trial, ironically he was one of a minority of 'clean' riders in the peloton. The day before the race began a soigneur of the Festina professional cycling team by the name of Willy Voet was stopped by customs officials on the Belgian-French border. Upon inspection of his vehicle they discovered a boot full of illegal performance enhancing drugs. Voets arrest and subsequent testimony initiated a police investigation which revealed a systematic doping programme for the riders which was wholeheartedly supported by the doctors, management and sponsors of the team. The fallout from the police investigation was far reaching with several other teams and numerous riders being implicated leading to many riders being arrested and team hotels being searched. The Festina and TVM teams were expelled from the race whilst several other teams voluntarily withdrew casting even more suspicion. Meanwhile the other riders left in the race staged a protest in support of their colleagues being treated like common criminals by refusing to race leading to the cancellation of that particular stage. There were calls from the media, politicians and even fans for the race to be stopped completely. The race director

Jean Marie LeBlanc managed to broker a deal with the remaining riders enabling La Grande Boucle to limp back to Paris where Marco Pantani was crowned the eventual winner. However the following year he was surrounded by controversy at the Giro d'Italia amid suspicions of drug abuse and expelled from the race on the penultimate day.

The 1999 edition was dubbed 'the Tour of redemption' after recovering cancer sufferer Lance Armstrong cruised to an emphatic victory. This led to a seven year autocratic rule of the race and the nickname 'Le Boss' all the while fending off accusations of using performance enhancing drugs which came to a head in the autumn of 2012 when USADA (United States Anti-Doping Agency) served him with a lifetime ban after several former colleagues testified against him. He was described by USADA as the perpetrator of *'the most sophisticated, professionalized and successful doping program the sport has ever seen.'* The Union Cycliste Internationale (UCI), cycling's governing body subsequently stripped Armstrong of his seven victories with the record books now showing as blank for the years 1999 to 2005. I don't have a problem with this but what I do resent is that the records still show other known dopers of that era as title holders such as Richard Virenque who was at the epicentre of the Festina scandal and belligerently denied any involvement as being the King of the Mountains winner. Maybe it's because he's French but the same rule needs to be applied to everyone or it just makes a complete mockery of the whole system.

People say they can remember where they were when they heard the news of the Twin Tower terrorist attack in New York, well as a huge Armstrong fan and 'believer' I can tell you exactly where I was when Pat McQuaid the head of the UCI gave the press conference denouncing Lance, I was watching it on the television in a hotel room in Phuket whilst enjoying my honeymoon with my lovely new wife Chriss. As sad and as pathetic as I know I now sound at the time I was gutted. My feelings were a mixture of shock and disbelief, how could Lance the cancer surviving miracle man have duped us all for so long. An inspiration to millions of people all over the world, people like my mother recovering from a stroke, wearing their yellow wrist bands believing in the ***LIVESTRONG*** motto and drawing strength from his heroic deeds on the bike. Turns out the 'trolls', Armstrong's derogatory nickname for non-believers and people suspicious of his success, journalists like Paul Kimmage and David Walsh unrelenting in their pursuit of Armstrong and the truth had been right all along. As for the so called televised confessional given to Oprah Winfrey well that only served to prove what an arrogant narcissistic megalomaniac the man actually is.

Much to the chagrin of the French people the last home winner of *their* race was way back in 1985 when Bernard Hinault won his fifth title to equal Miguel Indurain, Eddy Merckx and Jacques Anquetil with the most victories. In 2012 Sir Bradley Wiggins became the first ever British winner but has since been usurped by Chris Froome who won his third title in 2016, the fourth by a British rider in the last six years confirming Team Sky's dominance of the race. Maybe in the coming years he can join that elite club with five wins, he certainly has the potential.

So for 2016 the organisers of L'Etape, my third and final Challenge have chosen Stage 20 of the race starting in Megeve and finishing 146 kilometres away in Morzine Avoriaz in the Haute Savoie region of the Alps. Along the route riders will have to conquer four mountain passes including the Col des Aravis 1487 metres, Col de la Colombiere 1618 metres, Col de la Ramaz 1559 metres and finally Col de Joux Plane 1691 metres before descending to the finish in Morzine. In France all Cols or mountain passes are categorised according to their length, steepness and overall gain in altitude with the hardest climbs such as the Col du Galibier awarded a *Hors Categorie (HC)* meaning beyond catergorisation, others are rated one to four with four being the least difficult. The first climb of the day the Aravis is rated second category whilst the Colombiere and Ramaz are first category climbs saving the hardest until last the legendarily fearsome HC beyond category Joux Plane.

The charities we have chosen as recipients of our Challenge are:-

Jalon Valley Animal Rescue Centre

Jalon Valley ARC is a small rescue in Spain founded by British expats Jayne Webb and Sally Mason helping abandoned animals in the Jalon Valley, offering care and temporary fostering until rehoming is possible. Unfortunately the absence of animal welfare concern in Spain means these animals have very little chance of finding a home locally so ARC work with UK based rescues to help secure a safe future for them. Jayne and Sally operate this rescue purely out of their love for animals with the care and fostering happening mostly in their own homes. They also run a charity shop in the town of Jalon with the proceeds helping to contribute to the huge vet bills and other costs associated with the administration of ARC.

Kent Greyhound Rescue

Kent Greyhound Rescue is a registered charity based near Hythe in South East Kent. They find new homes for around 150 abandoned and unwanted greyhounds, lurchers and other sighthounds every year rehoming primarily throughout Kent but also in other counties across the UK (strict checks are carried out before any dog is rehomed, regardless of the location).

KGR receive no help or funding from the greyhound racing industry and their volunteers have the responsibility of fundraising every penny needed to ensure the charity can meet its financial obligations.

The vast majority of dogs arrive needing to be neutered or spayed, vaccinated and microchipped and most dogs also require dental and/or other medical treatment, as well as the usual worm and flea treatments. Some dogs need more help than others, but the average cost of rescuing each dog is approximately £500.

Due to their expenses they ask for a minimum donation of £250 when you adopt a dog, which goes towards the general running costs of the charity.

Most importantly KGR do not operate a rescue centre, which is open to the public. Instead the dogs wait for their new homes at either private boarding kennels near High Halstow or, ideally, in foster homes throughout Kent.

KGR are out nearly every weekend throughout the year fundraising. Volunteers do not get paid by KGR but give their time and efforts because they love the dogs, are passionate about animal welfare and want to find the KGR dogs new homes. The majority of them work full time and manage the charity and fundraising in their free time. KGR are incredibly grateful to their volunteers, fosterers and financial supporters because without them the charity would cease to exist.

Starfish Dog Rescue

Starfish is a small organisation which rescues and rehomes dogs and other pets.

They help people who are no longer able to keep their pets to find an alternative home for them, where they will be loved and cared for just as much as they have been in their original home. They also take in abandoned and stray animals working to find a permanent loving home for them.

Every dog rescued is important to them and from the moment a dog comes into their care they are committed to its welfare and happiness. This dog will be part of the Starfish doggy family and treated as one of its own and they are totally committed to helping this dog on towards its forever home for the rest of its life.

All dogs are placed in foster homes so they can be thoroughly assessed before rehoming. By living with a family, the dog gets used to the everyday routine it will face when rehomed. Foster carers are experienced dog lovers. They often have dogs, children, chickens and cats of their own and they are dedicated to helping the dogs get back to normal life.

All dogs are given a health check to make sure that there is no obvious condition which would prevent their rehoming. Starfish pay for emergency treatment when needed and vaccinate all their dogs. If a serious health condition is found, they will always let the new owners know before adoption.

Starfish believe in neutering as there are far too many unwanted dogs in the country and giving them a home is more urgent than breeding new puppies. They neuter all their dogs before rehoming them if funds allow and the dog is not too young or medically unfit for some reason. However if this happens to be the case as part of the contract the new owner must agree to do this at an appropriate time.

This practice is a non-negotiable condition of adoption for all Starfish dogs.

Another one of their policies involves microchipping all dogs. Microchipping is a very quick procedure which saves many a dog's life every year. A microchipped dog is far more likely to be reunited with its owners if it becomes lost or stolen.

Starfish also has an affiliate based in the Murcia region of Spain called Little Starfish run by a small group of ex-pat volunteers helping to rehome abandoned dogs and assessing their suitability for travel and eventual adoption in the UK whilst also supporting other animal rescue groups in the area.

Finally on the 1st of January 2016 ***Ritch's 3 Tour Challenge*** goes live.

Ride for Rescue

'The Tour of Flanders is unlike any other bike race in the world. It is, without question, the hardest one-day bike race ever created. What seems like a million corners, combined with twenty to thirty steep pitches and narrow roads, none of which go the same direction for more than a mile, all mix together to make it war on a bike. Flanders may as well be a different sport.'
George Hincapie (ex pro cyclist)

One morning about a week before I'm due to ride my first Challenge I wake up and as soon as I open my eyes the first sensation my brain registers is that I have a tickly throat. All athletes become so attuned to their bodies that they will recognise even the smallest of changes and for me a tickly throat is always the first symptom signifying the onset of a heavy cold. In my head, in my best Victor Meldrew voice I shout 'I don't believe it!' I've trained my arse off throughout winter in all conditions without so much as a sniffle and now it looks like on the eve of one of the biggest and most important races I'll ever ride that I'm coming down with manflu.

Bollocks! Fucking bollocks!

Instead of my customary strong coffee and breakfast bar I take a Lemsip with several paracetamol. Before a big event I usually have a week off training so that I can rest as much as possible in the hope that I'll have relatively fresh legs come race day. This is absolutely the case before my first Challenge as I ingest all manner of cold remedies hoping to stave off the dreaded lergy. Whether this helps or not I'm unsure, however my cold is manageable and I've certainly suffered a lot worse.

A rather inauspicious start to the Challenge nonetheless.

My best mate Alan is joining me for this Challenge which will be the first overseas cycling trip we've taken together for almost a decade so I'm really looking forward to his company. I'd invited him to do the *'hell of the north'* with me but he ruefully declined saying he couldn't get a pass off the missus for two consecutive weekends away, however I also think my tales of last years' experience may have scared him off somewhat.

Despite the inconvenience of an early start the journey across to Belgium is a pleasantly easy one and by mid-afternoon we find ourselves in an industrial area on the outskirts of Oudenaarde. We're sat in a very slow moving long queue of traffic as large numbers of cyclists zip past us, people are ditching cars anywhere that is possible and making out on foot for the registrations hall. Our satnav tells us we're about a mile away which at this rate could well take the best part of an hour so we pull into the nearest car park and join the crowds on foot like rats following the pied piper. A brisk fifteen minute walk through a rather grey, dull and characterless industrial estate brings us to the busy registrations hall which is basically what appears to be an empty warehouse outside which are numerous stalls selling all manner of cycling related merchandise. After signing on we receive our packs which include a coupon for a finishers medal which we duly collect from the first stall outside nearest to the entrance, Alan rather ruefully says 'Well there's no need to ride tomorrow now.' I have to agree with him it does seem somewhat anticlimactic.

Later that evening after a thoroughly enjoyable traditional Flemish stew dinner, the main ingredient being rabbit, I head for the bar whilst Alan, now teetotal for over a year goes up to the room to call his missus. I take a seat at the bar and order a large Leffe Blonde from the barmaid, for those of you who enjoy a brew you may be familiar with strong Belgian wheat beers and in my opinion this is one of the finest. As the barmaid pours my tasty beverage she asks me the reason for my visit to Ypres. 'I'm here for De Ronde' I happily reply 'tomorrow we're riding the sportive.' She nods appreciatively then pointing at my glass with an almost motherly tone instructs me 'Well don't have too many of those.' I give her a big cheesy grin holding the glass aloft in a toast and tell her 'Just one for the road.'

Saturday 2nd April 2016

It's another early start to make the hour long journey east across to Oudenaarde and it is still full dark when we leave the hotel. We eat breakfast in the car on the way consisting of bananas and energy bars washed down with energy drinks, hardly your traditional full English. During the journey there on an almost deserted motorway, which are more like our dual carriageways, we see in the distance two cars side by side taking up both lanes. Maybe a career in the armed forces and emergency services has given me a heightened sense of awareness for danger because as we approach the vehicles in front I have a disconcerting sense of foreboding. There's something about this picture that just doesn't feel right. I tell Alan, who's driving to keep his distance but he keeps closing the gap so I repeat myself more sternly this time. It seems there is some kind of altercation taking place as a person is leaning out of the car on the left gesticulating wildly at the other one. The same car suddenly swerves towards the other as though it's going to ram the other vehicle off the road. Both vehicles brake suddenly then speed up all the while moving erratically along the carriageway. This scenario plays out in front of us like a scene from a Hollywood action movie for several minutes before the car that seems to be the victim of the road rage incident suddenly swerves right off the motorway and down the next slip road followed at high speed by the main protagonist. As we carry on over a bridge they disappear out of sight veering wildly across the road brake lights flashing in unison.

By the time we reach Oudenaarde it's beginning to get light as we're directed by a marshal into a very busy parking area. People dressed in lycra are everywhere engaged in unloading their vehicles and readying their two wheel steads for the coming adventure. Alan and I join them like worker ants foraging around the nest. I stuff the pockets of my *'British Cycling'* jersey with gels and energy bars hoping I've brought enough to see me through the entire ride, the organisers provide food and drink at various 'feed zones' around the course but I prefer to use the brand I like. There's a chill to the morning air but at least it's dry with a fair forecast predicted all day long. We follow the signs down to an open start and after the obligatory pre ride selfie we unceremoniously get underway.

After a gentle loop round the Schelde river the course heads east away from Oudenaarde to the first climb of the day the Wolvenberg first used by the race in 1999, which despite a maximum gradient of

17% at half a mile long with an average gradient of 6% is more of an aperitif of what's to come. I'm sure most riders found it pretty easy but in my weakened state I found myself blowing a bit on the steepest pitches.

When I train I usually like at least a nice easy twenty minutes spin to start with just to raise my body temperature and get my legs warmed up however today even after an hours riding I'm still not feeling it. I'm feeling hot but not in a good sweaty way due to the effects of physical exertion and if I had to guess I'd say I'm only about 70% fit suffering from a slight fever with a mild chest infection.

A sharp left hand turn off the main road leads us on to the Molenberg, which is a berg in the true spirit of De Ronde. It is narrow, I actually thought we had gone off the route and were going up somebody's driveway, deceptively steep and cobbled. Whoever told me the cobbles here were better than those at Roubaix must have been pulling my leg because they certainly don't seem so to me, the realisation quickly hits me that there's only one thing worse than flat cobbles and that's cobbles that go uphill. They protrude at random angles with gaps big enough to snag your wheel whilst the adverse camber slopes horrendously away from you making the steeper part of the climb even harder. As the road bends sharply to the right into the steepest pitch of the berg Alan comes flying past me, as his short skinny but muscular legs piston furiously he quickly opens a gap on me as I shout after him 'Gas it wanker!' Fortunately this juddering ordeal is short lived as the climb is only about a quarter of a mile in length.

As we ride away from the Molenberg either my demeanour or pallor or maybe both must be causing Alan some concern as he asks me if I'm alright.

'I feel like dog shit' I tell him matter of fact.

'We can stop if you need to?' he offers sympathetically.

'Nah you're alright if I stop I might not get going again' I reply despondently 'just knock a rev off eh?'

In cycling parlance to knock a rev off means to slow down a bit usually to assist a rider who is finding the pace difficult to keep up with. Given the way I'm feeling I'm actually beginning to wonder if

I'll be able to finish this ride. Then I remind myself why I'm here, why I'm doing this, my suffering is insignificant in comparison to that which Galgos like Spencer and Podencos like Olive are subjected to over in Spain. This is all the motivation I need to suck it up and keep turning the pedals first left then right, one after another, failure is absolutely not an option.

After two long secteurs of pave at Paddestraat and Haaghoek which I would rate as 4 star we arrive at the next climb of the day, the Leberg which fortunately is asphalted as is the next climb of Berendries a couple of miles later. These climbs may be fairly short but because they are so steep and follow each other in such close proximity they sap the strength from your legs, despite this at some point I'm not sure when but I actually start to feel much better settling into a nice steady rhythm. If nothing else the names of these climbs are suitably impressive as we conquer the Valkenberg then the Eikenberg on the way to the most iconic climb of the race the Koppenberg.

This climb despite being only half a mile long is incredibly narrow barely passable by a small car and extremely steep including ramps of over 1 in 5 with very irregular cobbles which are often wet and muddy. As we approach the climb we can see it is virtually dead straight as it heads upwards disappearing into a copse of trees, I attempt to increase my pace by upping my cadence as we pass the houses on either side of the road. Imagine this being on your doorstep. As I reach the trees the cobbles become much rougher with the road getting increasingly steeper which forces me out of the saddle, yet again Alan surges past on my left. The etiquette of cycling suggests riders should keep to the right thereby allowing faster moving cyclists plenty of room to pass, however this climb becomes so steep and narrow that riders end up funnelling into a bottleneck like grains of sand in an hourglass. For the first time it strikes me the vast number of participants in this event. Where the climb is at its steepest is also where you'll find the roughest, wettest and muddiest cobbles. I'll be honest even if I'd been the only rider there I seriously doubt I'd have made it up because I'm forced to sit down to stop the rear wheel slipping on the muddy pave which means I can't exert enough pressure even in the smallest gear to turn the pedals over. As it is I'm forced to stop anyway due to the crowds in front of me whilst some hardy souls are still attempting to ride up shouting at people to get out of their way. The banks on each side are incredibly high with almost vertical walls which I use to stop myself falling over as I'm forced to unclip and dismount. If trying to ride on these cobbles was difficult attempting to walk up them pushing a bike in cleated cycling shoes is almost impossible, I'd have an easier time in the wife's high heels for sure. Staggering and weaving like a pisshead on his way home from the pub I struggle to maintain my balance whilst negotiating the crowds for about thirty metres before I find a suitable opportunity to get back on my bike. Remounting, I push off as hard as I can quickly clipping in and grind my way up the final steep arc to the summit of the climb. I soon reunite with Alan who has suffered the same fate as I did, somebody in front of him lost traction and slipped thereby having to unclip which inevitably caused him to do likewise.

Am I disappointed that I didn't make it up the Koppenberg. Absolutely not at all no, I'd read on social media in the days prior to the sportive that a number of pros during their reconnaissance rides had had to dismount, so I consider myself to be in pretty good company.

The smooth tarmac soon gives way to another long secteur of pave at Mariaborrestraat which I grant you is much easier to ride than the stones of Roubaix. We've been riding now for about three hours having covered the best part of fifty miles which leads us into the climb of the Taaienberg which literally translated means 'tough mountain'. This climb reminds me of the earlier Molenberg as the cobbles are very bumpy and ramps up pretty steeply with a sharp right hand bend except it is significantly longer. After the bend there is a concrete drain on the far right hand side which riders are making a beeline toward. I'm stuck on the cobbles in the midst of several riders waiting for a suitable gap to get across to this luxuriously smooth strip of road when there is a distinctive mechanical ping from the rider next to me and I feel an object fly past me. I look to my right to see that his seat clamp has just snapped, the saddle now hanging limply from the seat post. This happened to me a couple of years ago just outside Preston whilst I was riding to Blackburn to pick up my car and I can tell you that last ten miles was horrendously hard not being able to sit down. Next time you go cycling just try staying out of the saddle for as long as you can, it'll have your quads screaming with lactic acid overload before you know it. We still have a very difficult thirty miles or so left to ride which means unless this guy has a spare, which is extremely unlikely, can locate a bike shop or encounters a good Samaritan his race is well and truly over.

Two fairly long but relatively easy tarmac climbs of Kaperij and Kanarieberg which we affectionately call the 'Canaryberg' bring us to the final feeding zone of the sportive so we pull in for refreshments and a comfort break. There is only approximately twenty miles left to the finish from here but we still have two of the most difficult climbs to negotiate, the much revered and iconic Oude Kwaremont and Paterberg before we return to Oudenaarde.

We are soon back on our way and after a couple of longer but more gradual asphalted climbs we are headed towards the climactic finale where in the pro race the winning move is often made. Unlike the pros who take in a loop which sees them tackle these last two climbs twice fortunately we only have to struggle up them the once. In the distance we can see several huge brilliant white marquees dominating the skyline which are the hospitality areas on the Kwaremont. On the approach to the base of the climb the road is sectioned off with barriers and manned by marshals with signs of tortoises indicated to go left and hares to the right. After a brief check of our race numbers we are directed to the right naturally before executing a right turn onto the lower slopes. At almost a mile and a half in length the Oude Kwaremont (or Kluisberg as the climb is actually called) is the longest climb in the region of Flanders and has been a mainstay of the race ever since 1974.

Fortunately the lower third of the climb is on tarmac which allows me to generate some speed and get into a nice rhythm before the cobbles and steeper pitches begin. The cobbles are comparatively smooth to begin with but as I reach the first steep section they deteriorate as a distinctive bulging crown has caused them to subside, whilst the road significantly narrows with the high banks closing in on you giving a palpable sense of claustrophobia. I stay in the saddle, pushing hard on the pedals determined not to have to stop thankful that the stones are dry. I'm aware of numerous spectators along the roadside cheering us on as the gradient eases passing several buildings before it ramps up again which forces me out of the saddle. Breathing hard, struggling to turn the pedals over I'm praying for the end to come. As the bike judders and bounces on the rough surface my upper body absorbing the vibrations I have to sit down to control the bike my pace slowing even further. With one last huge effort through gritted teeth, shoulders bobbing exaggeratedly from side to side I finally reach the summit. The route veers left continuing on the cobbles but fortunately now on the flat for several hundred metres where Alan catches me up before we hit blessedly smooth tarmac again. One down, one to go.

The very last climb of the race, the Paterberg was until 1986 an unmade road which a local farmer paved with cobblestones to encourage De Ronde to pass by his property, this is how fanatical Flandrians are about *their* race. It has been used every year since then becoming the show-stopping finale from 2012 onwards. In the run up to my first Challenge I'd been watching clips on YouTube from previous editions of De Ronde to get a feel for what I'd be letting myself in. As the motto of my old army unit 'the Green Slime' (Intelligence Corps) states in latin, **manui dat cognition vires** which translates as 'knowledge gives strength to the arm' or in this case the legs.

We hit a very fast descent which I can see in the foreground ends in a very sharp ninety degree right hand turn, this is *IT* the start of the Paterberg. Alan is behind me whilst I have a bit of open road in front, perfect I'm determined to nail this. As I rapidly approach the right hand bend I get my gears sorted then brake sharply scrubbing off just enough speed to make the corner. I make a textbook exit out of the corner and the cobbles which are in pretty good condition start immediately but I barely notice as I hammer the pedals. There are a number of slower moving riders in front of me who I quickly negotiate by shouting ''a droite'' (to the right) at them as I pass. About halfway up this straight, short but very steep climb the incline starts to bite so with a flick of the left brake lever I engage the small chainring attempting to keep my cadence high. Another couple of clicks and I'm in my smallest gear standing out of the saddle pushing against the gravitational twenty percent incline as many riders succumb to the steepness of the slope wearily pushing their bikes on foot. I'm almost forced to stop when a slower rider in front veers across my line but I have enough power left in the tank to swerve round him and keep my momentum going. As I'm about to run out of gas I can see the summit just ahead which gives me enough motivation to make one final lunge to the top of the climb before turning left off the cobbles back onto the flat. I did it, I'm absolutely euphoric. I look over my right shoulder to see where Alan is almost colliding with a guy who has suddenly stopped at the side of the road. I acknowledge his shouts of alarm thinking to myself 'Well get off the fucking road then!' as Alan emerges from the crowds who loiter annoyingly about the summit and rejoins me.

We're now less than ten miles from the finish and a short descent brings us to the scenic main road leading back to Oudenaarde. A pretty fast moving train of riders comes past us so I up my pace to jump on the back of the group. At this speed I should be able to make my prerace target of five and a half hours. After a couple of minutes I look over my shoulder to check Alan is ok only to see him several hundred yards back down the road. I have two choices, I can carry on motoring to the finish or I can wait for my friend. As far as I'm concerned you don't leave your mates so I sit up and gently spin the pedals until he catches me up.

'You alright pal' I ask.

'Yeah, just feeling it a bit now' he replies almost apologetically.

Alan is a decent rider, strong on climbs but probably lacking a bit of power on the flat due to his body size, he's about nine stone pissed wet through with the physique of a pre-pubescent boy, especially now when fatigue and the lack of training miles are starting to show. Due to work commitments and pressure from a less than understanding wife Alan unfortunately struggles to put the miles in. We cruise along on the flat in silence enjoying the satisfaction of success. The final kilometre to the official finish is dead straight and as the banner approaches we congratulate each other shaking hands as we cross the line.

One Challenge complete, two to go.

Strava Data for Ronde Van Vlaanderen Cyclo 2016 :-
Distance   81.5 miles
Moving time   5 hours 33 minutes
Average speed   14.5mph
Elevation gain   4803ft

In the three months since the Challenge started we had managed to raise £1,075.00. Immediately following completion of the first Challenge we received a further £195 in donations.

Here's what some of our supporters had to say-

'Yayyy!!! That looks flippin horrendous tho- enjoy your beers'

'Well done Ritch, what an achievement'

'Great stuff Ritch considering you were under the weather!'

Race Day Remembrance

'Are you fond of cycling? If so why not cycle for the King'
Extract from First World War Army recruiting poster

Sunday is a Carlsberg day, probably.

As I mentioned earlier I'd decided for the first Challenge to base myself in Ypres so that I could combine riding the sportive with paying my respects to relatives that were killed in the First World War. By coincidence it transpires that Alans' paternal Great Grandfather was also killed during the war and happens to be buried in a cemetery on the outskirts of Ypres. Alan also reveals that he'll be the first member of his family to visit the grave which fills me with a sense of pride at not only bringing about the visit but in joining him to pay remembrance. Given the tragically high number of British casualties many from working class towns such as Accrington where all of Alans' descendants hail from I shouldn't be surprised by the coincidence.

Accrington is undoubtedly one of the most famous towns in England for several reasons. Having lived there for many years before moving to the Fylde coast I still feel a strong sense of warmth and affinity for the town. Anyone of a certain generation will remember the famously comedic milk advert produced by the Milk Marketing Board featuring two adolescent Liverpool fans with one telling the other that Ian Rush, all-time leading goal scorer for Liverpool football club, has advised him that if he drinks two glasses of milk a day he might be good enough to play for Accrington Stanley.

'Accrington Stanley, who are they?' is the response in a very strong high pitched scouse accent.

'Exactly!'

Accrington Stanley was formed in 1891 being one of the founding fathers of the football League but unfortunately went into liquidation in 1966 having to resign from the League halfway through the season. Two years later the club was reformed but wasn't to play professional league football again until 2006 and despite ongoing financial issues still play today in the modern day League Two.

Another reason for the global fame of the town is Accrington brick or NORI as it's colloquially known due to the word IRON being accidentally stamped backwards in the brick moulds. Accrington brick was produced from 1887 until the closure of the works in 2008, with its usage becoming widespread due to the strength and hardness of the brick because of the high iron content in the clay used during the firing process. The bricks were also acid resistant which meant they were ideal for lining flues and chimneys which led to them being used at several power stations such as Battersea and Sellafield. Another feature of the brick was their distinctive reddish colour, again because of the iron content, with an extremely high proportion of domestic dwellings and commercial sites being built using Accrington brick. In fact the term 'redbrick university' in reference to several universities founded in major industrial cities comes from the Accrington brick that was used to build them.

However the town is probably most famous because of the battalion that was recruited at the outbreak of the First World War known as the 'Accrington Pals'. These battalions gained the moniker 'Pals' as they were made up of fathers, brothers, uncles, cousins, friends and neighbours all from the same town who worked, drank and played together. Accrington was the smallest town in Britain to raise an entire battalion. Officially recorded as the 11th Battalion, East Lancashire Regiment the Accrington Pals were all but wiped out in the opening minutes of the Battle of the Somme on the 1st July 1916 the bloodiest battle in British Military history accounting for a devastating sixty thousand casualties. The memorial to the Pals in Serre, France where they 'went over the top' is a three sided wall, made appropriately of course from Accrington brick.

Alans' Great Grandfather wasn't a member of the Pals. Private Herbert Akred served with the 8th Battalion South Lancashire Regiment when he was killed on the 22nd July 1917 during the Battle of Messines and is buried in Belgian Battery Corner cemetery just over a mile west of Ypres. We find the cemetery with relative ease thanks to the sat nav, leaving the warmth of the car we brave the chill of the damp overcast morning. I don't know about Alan, he's a man of few words and reveals his emotions even less but visiting our fallen heroes always makes me feel rather melancholy and brings a tear to my eye. As with all the military cemeteries this one is immaculately kept, credit due to the remarkable work of the Commonwealth War Graves Commission and with just over five hundred graves it is reasonably intimate being flanked on two sides by residential dwellings. It doesn't take us long to locate his Great Grandfathers grave and after the obligatory photograph I leave him to pay his respects whilst I explore the rest of the cemetery, as always astounded by the diversity of names, regiments and nationalities on the ghostly white pristine headstones.

A short drive takes us to West Vleteren where we negotiate a short dirt track which leads to Dozinghem Military Cemetry to visit my Great Grandfathers brother in law. Private Andrew Lee served with the 15th Battalion Cheshire Regiment, he died of wounds on the 11th November 1917 and so the family story goes he told his mother when he was leaving to join the war that he wouldn't be back. This is my third visit and as on both previous occasions I'm struck by the peace and tranquillity as I listen to the morning birdsong. Despite my other visits it still takes several minutes to find him amongst the other three and a half thousand graves with the lines from Rupert Brooke's poem 'The Soldier' seemingly more profound than ever.

'If I should die, think only this of me
That there's some corner of a foreign field
That is forever England.'

Ironically whilst wandering amongst the headstones I happen across another Private Lee who served with the Army Cyclist Corps, the hairs on the back of my neck stand on end. The Army Cyclist Corps was formed in 1915 becoming an invaluable asset used primarily for reconnaissance and communications work as the bicycle was lighter, quieter and much easier to support logistically than horses. The corps was later disbanded in 1920 as motorised vehicles became prevalent.

After our Sunday morning of remembrance we spend the afternoon in Oudenaarde, the spiritual home of Belgian cycling. The impressive gothic town square has been turned into a parking lot for the professional team buses awaiting the return of these warriors of the road. For any cycling fan paying a visit to the town the museum Centrum Ronde Van Vlaanderen is a must see, the paltry sum of eight euros grants you access to an interestingly interactive experience taking you on a whirlwind tour of the history of the race over the years with an array of physical artefacts on display.

We emerge from the museum into the glorious sunshine of a perfect spring afternoon and as we head towards the race finish line several female professional cyclists pass us in dribs and drabs heading in the opposite direction towards the team buses parked in the town square. Disappointedly I remark to Alan that I think we may have missed the women's race, which I am a big fan of.

Women's cycling has come a long way since the bicycle became a vehicle for the emancipation of women back in the late 1800s, one such woman was the American Annie Londonderry who 'cycled round the world' during the course of 1894-5 to highlight not only what women are capable of but to also challenge the values of society at that time. Despite this impressive feat it wasn't until 1984, almost a hundred years later that a female cycling event was held in the Olympics, the women's road race which was won by another American, Connie Carpenter. In the same year the very first women's Tour de France or Grande Boucle Feminine was introduced albeit much shorter than the men's race at between ten to fifteen stages, with Jeannie Longo of France becoming the first three time winner and one of the greatest female cyclists ever who successfully competed well into her 50s.

As women's racing grew in popularity more events, usually mirroring the men's calendar, were scheduled which led to the UCI Women Road World Cup being created which was held from 1998 to 2015 subsequently being replaced by the UCI Women's World Tour to accommodate the rapid growth of the sport.

Fortunately we actually haven't missed the ladies race, the girls that have cycled passed us have already abandoned the race and are making their way back to the team buses for an early bath. We reach the 'Fan Zone', free entry by the way, in time to watch on the big screen as Britain's own Lizzie Armistead resplendent in the stripes of the World road race champion makes the race winning attack on the

Paterberg which she makes look a lot easier than I did yesterday to be fair. We have a great view directly opposite the finish line as Lizzie crosses the line arms aloft in victory. Chapeau.

As the crowd grows considerably, with the smell of cooking hot dogs permeating the air and copious amounts of beer being consumed Alan remarks 'I knew cycling was big over here but I didn't know it was *this* big!' We watch as the great cobble specialist Fabian 'Spartacus' Cancellara in his retirement year tries in vain to hold the wheel of World road race champion Peter Sagan who also makes the winning move over the Paterberg and eventually soloes to victory showboating across the finish line pulling his now customary wheelie in celebration.

Correct me if I'm wrong but I'm pretty sure that this is the first race where both the men's and women's World champion have won their respective event.

That evening we round off an almost perfect weekend by attending the Last Post Ceremony at the Menin Gate Memorial to the Missing in Ypres. Every evening at exactly 8pm since 1928 buglers from the local Fire Brigade have sounded the Last Post in gratitude towards those who gave their lives in the fight for Belgium's freedom.

This is particularly poignant for me as my maternal Great Grandfathers name, Private Arthur Hamilton 3rd Battalion (The Diehards) Middlesex Regiment who was killed at the Battle of Neuve Chapelle on 11th March 1915 is etched in stone on panel 51.

Never Say Never Again

'Paris Roubaix is the best race in the World, it knocks spots off the Tour de France.'
Sir Bradley Wiggins CBE (Britain's greatest ever cyclist and Tour de France winner 2012)

'hell' noun >UK /hel/ an extremely unpleasant or difficult place, situation or experience

After travelling back from Belgium on Monday I only have three days at home to recover and prepare for my second Challenge before heading to France on Friday. This time I'll be flying solo which doesn't really concern me for several reasons; I've ridden this event before, I do most of my cycling by myself and have travelled across France on my own in the past. At the risk of sounding ungrateful I wasn't completely happy with Murphs planning and organisation of last year's trip and know that I can do much better, after all I've had plenty of experience of organising trips from the years when I used to follow the Tour de France with Alan.

The first change to my itinerary from last year's trip is that I'll be travelling to France using the Eurotunnel service rather than by ferry. This has significant advantages in that the train service runs from Folkestone, half an hour less drive than going to Dover, there are three trains every hour and in most circumstances you are able to board the next available train. The embarkation and offload process is much quicker but perhaps most critically the crossing only takes half an hour, a third of the time the ferry takes. Last year we lost over three hours waiting for the next ferry and during the crossing to Calais which had the knock on effect of us hitting rush hour traffic around Lille. To be perfectly honest I'm surprised travellers still use the ferry service given the far superior logistical experience afforded by the tunnel.

An early start from Blackpool and a happily hassle free journey sees me arrive at the velodrome in Roubaix by half past two that afternoon. I manage to parallel park my Ford Fiesta into the tiniest gap possible between two cars receiving a thumbs up off the female driver of the car behind. Whether she's impressed with my reverse parking skill or just relieved I haven't bumped her car I'm not sure.

The registrations area is situated inside the Velodrome Jean Stablinski, a modern multi-purpose indoor velodrome built in 2012 named after the former professional who was the catalyst for the use of the Arenberg secteur having known of its existence from his early career working in the mine there. Within minutes I leave the impressively glass fronted building with a white envelope in my hand, I don't bother opening it as I already know what's inside. I wander through the stalls selling all kinds of colourful cycling merchandise and there she is in all her faded glory the Mecca of cycling. Passing the huge cobblestone memorial donated by 'Les Amis de Paris Roubaix' commemorating the one hundredth edition of the race in 2002 I stroll through the open iron gates onto the concrete boards and turn right following the anti-clockwise direction round the track that the race takes. I linger to marvel at the steepness of the boards on the apex of the final bend before walking across the thin strip of dark blue tape marking the finish line opposite the small covered seated stand.

Crossing the grassed infield area where on Sunday another champion will be immortalised I head towards the Velo Club Roubaix which is basically a small bar come shop. Above the busy bar are the names of all the past winners chalked on blackboards, the smell of strong coffee and stale beer fills my nostrils as I approach the shops glass counter. On display are what I have come for, small replica trophies of a cobblestone mounted on a wooden plinth as received by the winner of the race. In pigeon French I request two trophies one for this year and the other for finishing the event last year which I never had the opportunity to purchase, the assistant asks me to choose the ones I'd like. Unsurprisingly I pick the two largest roughest looking ones, I am however surprised at their weight as she hands me a musette bag containing them.

Exiting the bar there is one last thing I have come to see so I begin my search of the decrepit concrete buildings across the courtyard behind the Velo Club. I'm beckoned into one of these featureless buildings by a bespectacled French woman who in perfect English asks me if I'd like to see the museum enticing me in by the free entry. Centrum Van Vlaanderen it certainly is not but there is still enough bike porn and historical artefacts from the race to entertain the eye especially the old cobbles and marker stones taken from the secteurs of pave. On the way out I encounter the same lady whom I ask where the notoriously iconic shower block can be found but she apologetically tells me that today it is are closed.

As I'm about to make my way back to the car I see a steel fire door open and several people emerge from inside. My intuition tells me this is the shower block so I dash over catching the door before it closes on me. He who dares wins Rodders. And, I'm not disappointed. To say the facilities are basic is a complete understatement. It is indeed as I've read very much like a cattle shed with milking stalls. Everything is made of cold grey concrete apart from a small wooden bench in every stall and the metal of taps and shower heads. Each stall has a brass plaque engraved with the name of a previous winner and the year or years of their victories. Whilst I'm sat in the stall bearing Bernard Hinaults name, who famously said 'Paris Roubaix is a race for dickheads' I imagine the room full of dirty sweaty bodies, steam hanging in the air misting up the windows, the sound of running water and the chatter of riders reminiscing about their day in hell filling the stiflingly moist warm air. It's absolutely fabulous.

All in all it's been a very successful start to the second Challenge and if the rest of the weekend particularly tomorrow goes in the same vein I'll be extremely happy. The most stressful part is the twenty minute drive negotiating the traffic and one way streets on the outskirts of Lille to find the hotel which is a French equivalent of a Travelodge situated in the residential area of Wasquehal. By nine that evening I've prepped my gear for tomorrow, been fed, watered and ready to get some much needed sleep. Most importantly it's reassuringly quiet.

Saturday 9th April 2016

My alarm is set for four in the morning, although it's not the best night's sleep I've ever had it's a damn sight better than the night I experienced before last year's race and I wake feeling relatively refreshed. Preparation after all is key.

Fortunately I've become well accustomed to sleep deprivation, a career with the emergency services does that for you but even more fortunately I'm very much a morning person. This also includes my toilet habits, regular as clockwork within minutes of waking up I will usually feel the need for a bowel movement. Last year I had to suffer the ignominy of using the cramped lavatory on a moving coach squatting over the bowl desperately trying not to soil my bib shorts. No such embarrassment this year in the privacy of my hotel bathroom.

Managing to find a parking spot just before the right turn into the velodrome I scan the road in both directions searching for the convoy of coaches to no avail. The car behind mine also has British registration plates, the two occupants busy removing their bikes from the boot. I walk over to them to see if they know where the transport to Busigny can be found. After a brief exchange I'm informed that they are situated about half a mile away on the carpark of a local shopping mall. Despite having no lights I mount my bike and follow the numerous other cyclists heading away from the velodrome.

There must be at least fifty identical looking coaches lined up like dominoes in the glare of the artificial street lights, I'm again impressed by how well the logistics for this event are handled. In the organised chaos I manage to find the coach I've been allocated to and join the queue of people waiting to have their machines loaded into the bike carrier. I'm of fairly average build and height but the bloke in front of me is a man mountain casting a huge shadow over me. He looks familiar from his profile then as he turns to face me I recognise him straight away, it's only Martin Johnson CBE former captain of the England rugby union team that were victorious at the 2003 World Cup. It looks like he's trimmed down considerably and he seems aware that I've recognised him, not that I'm staring or anything. He acknowledges me so I reply as casually as possible 'Alright pal.'

After watching the coach driver carefully stow my bike I climb aboard choosing a seat towards the rear of the coach, Martin and his companions have commandeered the back row of seats. Two English lads board choosing to sit directly behind me and proceed to chat throughout the whole journey. I was hoping for a bit of peace and quiet, some mental solitude to prepare for what I'm about to undertake but one of the pair is that kind of really annoying individual that just loves the sound of their own voice. I'd have moved seats but the coach is almost full by now. Oh woe is me. As I try to zone out the white noise from behind me I watch with a wry, knowing smile as a bloke a couple of rows ahead and across the aisle meticulously applies tape to his hands like a boxer before a prize fight.

This year I've made the decision that I'm not going to tape up my hands as I feel it didn't actually make much difference, the blisters I suffered being positive evidence of this. Instead I have a brand new pair of snug tight fitting gloves that my wife bought me which I'm hoping will prevent most of the chaffing. On the way down to Busigny I eat my usual pre ride breakfast consisting of a couple of energy bars and a handful of bananas, I recall Moose commenting last year that he'd never seen anyone eat so much before a race. I'd heard the legendary tales of Moose taking only a solitary gel on the bike lap of an ironman course, no wonder there isn't an ounce of fat on him. Know your body and know what works for you is what I say.

When we reach Busigny dawn is breaking into what looks like and has been forecast as an almost perfect day for cycling, the sun is breaking through white cumulus cloud and while there's a typically spring morning chill I suspect it will warm up reasonably as the day progresses. However most critically for a day out on the pave of northern France is that it's dry.

We must be one of the first coaches to arrive as by the time I've collected my bike and made my way to the official start there are perhaps only fifty or so cyclists waiting to begin the race. I check my watch and see it's only twenty past seven, the official start being at half past. Some riders are chatting excitedly or taking selfies whilst others myself included are waiting in silent contemplation despite the boom boom of euro pop coming from the sound system. It's fair to say I'm nervous, if I wasn't there'd be something wrong, though I'm not nearly as nervous as I was last year. Finally the wait is over and with a wave of the marshal's flag we roll across the start line.

Making our way west away from the village I notice the start of the route has changed from last year as we pass the Busigny Communal Military Cemetry strung out in single file on our way to the traditional first secteur of pave at Troisvilles a Inchy. My plan is to ride how I rode the second half of last year's race by taking it fairly steady on the pave then trying to make up time on the tarmac where possible, bearing in mind I'm still recovering from the manflu I was suffering from at Flanders and still not quite one hundred percent fit yet. However this rapidly goes out the window as nervous adrenaline soon takes over approaching the very first secteur. This year though I've cast frugality aside like an old shoe and invested in the 27mm Roubaix tyres as advocated by Murph so we're about to see if they'll make a difference.

Memories flood back instantly as we hit those first cobbles. Being in the first group to set off has the advantage that there's less detritus to negotiate however I pass several riders who have stopped and are walking back to collect their lost belongings. After a couple more secteurs have been negotiated I end up following a pair of female riders from Germany, well I'm guessing that's where they are from judging by the writing on their jerseys. I'm also guessing that they have ridden the cobbles before as I have trouble keeping up with their smooth powerful style on the pave but am quick to catch their wheel back on the tarmac. Despite one of them riding a cyclocross bike and the other a full suspension mountain bike I'm willing to overlook this as the view is rather agreeable. Let's be honest though who wouldn't rather follow a pair of shapely bronze calves and a pert lycra clad derriere with long blond pigtails flying in the wind than a hairy arsed fireman. At the first feed station however they swing off and I'm left riding alone again.

Roubaix is unlike any other event that I've ridden and not just because of the cobbles. What makes the 'hell of the north' unique is that in other events I've participated in there are usually numerous groups of cyclists on the road with whom you can ride which not only increases your speed but has the massive advantage of saving you enormous amounts of energy. Due to the nature of the terrain at Roubaix it literally is every man for himself, riders are strung out in single file in their personal battle against the pave with the odd group of a handful of riders here and there. The cobbles begin after just a few miles from leaving Busigny and once they start you are never off them for a sustained period until you reach the outskirts of Roubaix.

After a couple more secteurs have been carefully negotiated I find myself riding on the wheel of an English girl, the large white lettering on her bib tights stating **GREAT BRITAIN** gives the game away. I emerge from my position of shelter and engage her in small talk.

'How are you enjoying Roubaix?' I ask.

'I'm not!' is her somewhat clipped and tight lipped reply.

'This is my second time, I was here last year' I tell her proudly.

'Are you insane?' she asks incredulously

I give her an abridged version of why I'm here. Ironically it turns out my new riding companion is studying chemistry literally down the road from me at the university in Preston. She tells me that she's here with her father who has disappeared up the road somewhere, so much for chivalry. If I was here with my daughter there's absolutely no way I would leave her but like I said the pave completely levels the playing field. As we ride along chatting the streets start to look very familiar and I realise that we are on the approach to Arenberg Sure enough the iconic pithead machinery looms into view keeping its sombre menacing vigil over the forest as if to warn of the dangers lurking there.

Hoping to sound fatherly rather patronising I tell my companion 'This is it, Arenberg! It starts off downhill so it's pretty fast but the cobbles are absolutely atrocious and very slippery. Be careful!'

With what is supposed to be a ladies first gesture I allow her to go to the front and she leads us into 'hell'.

Unlike last year the footpath has been completely sectioned off with barriers but believe it or not my intention is to ride every single stone this time round. Keeping to the right hand side which tends to be drier my instinct for self-preservation kicks in and I calmly squeeze the brakes to keep my speed in check, this unfortunately increases the vibrations from the front wheel. I bounce along absorbing the pummelling from the pave desperately seeking the smoothest line as a young lad on my left cries out in shock 'This is fucking mental, I'm never doing this again!'

Laughing like a mad man I shout back 'That's what I said last year!'

Further ahead in my peripheral vision I notice my companion has stopped and dismounted for some reason. Maybe she's punctured or even worse crashed, do I stop to check she's okay, of course not this is *hell*. Pushing on I'm trying to keep my wheels on a thin strip of grass without hitting the protruding legs of the barriers doing my utmost to avoid the unforgiving cobbles. After what feels like forever but in reality is actually only a few minutes I see the finish banner and for the second time emerge thankfully unscathed from the terrifying forest.

Turning left onto the main road heading back parallel to the forest I notice that I feel quite tired which fills me with a sense of trepidation knowing that I'm not even half way yet with seventeen secteurs still to overcome. Having said that I'm still recuperating from the heavy cold which slowed me down at Flanders the weekend before. I manage to get on the wheel of four guys on mountain bikes who despite the fat tyres have got a decent lick on and take a breather drafting in their slipstream, they might as well be of some use.

It's relentless………..cobbles, more cobbles, then more cobbles, then even more cobbles.

There's virtually no respite from the incessant shuddering, juddering, bouncing vibrations as the smooth road sections between secteurs of pave never seem to last for longer than a few minutes of riding. I pass one of the places where I punctured last year recalling the bridleway heading off into the distance at ninety degrees to the cobbles, the new tyres seem to be working a treat up to now or maybe I've just been lucky. I'm not a superstitious person but if I dared release my vice like grip on the handlebars to keep my fingers crossed I certainly would. As if to remind me that successfully riding the pave is as much about luck as skill there's a loud exaggerated hiss from over my left shoulder, a noise not to dissimilar to air brakes on a truck going off, as the rider behind me suffers a puncture.

The weather is almost perfect for a long hard day in the saddle, it's quite cool but the sun is doing its best to burn off the light cloud cover. Despite being dry it's not unusual for some areas of pave to still be wet, Arenberg being notoriously slippery. On the following secteur I'm riding in the right hand gutter on a strip of hard dirt about six inches wide doing my best to avoid the sharp protruding edges of the stones. Maybe it's because I'm tired or not concentrating, or both but before I can take evasive action to avoid it I hit a patch of wet, greasy mud. The front wheel sharply veers uncontrollably to the left and in the skip of a heartbeat I'm airborne. I'm instantly thrown over the handlebars onto the grass verge on my right, thankfully it's a soft yet albeit prickly landing as I fall into some nettles. If I'd fallen the other way I might not have been as fortunate, I'd read how last year somebody had fractured their scapula falling onto the pave and when he asked an elderly local man for assistance the response had been 'What would a Flandrien do?' He eventually rode on and reached the velodrome before heading straight for the hospital. To add insult to injury as I get to my feet I slip down the banking into the drainage ditch ending up with very wet dirty feet. Riders rattle past as I check myself and my bike over making sure I haven't lost anything during my tumble. I doubt my fall would have received many marks for artistic merit but I'm sure it was rather entertaining for the riders following me.

Now I've had the full experience.

I pull into the final feed station at Templeuve for a rest as much as refreshing my water bottles. From here there's still over twenty miles and seven secteurs of pave to ride before reaching the hallowed velodrome. After about fifteen minutes as I'm about to head back out onto the course my acquaintance from Preston is just arriving. We exchange a few words, I tell her about my lucky fall and she explains what had happened in the forest that the rider in front of her crashed which brought her to a standstill. There's still no sign of her father. I wish her luck and ride off, within less than half a mile I'm back on the unrelenting cobbles.

It seems like time is speeding up because I'm certain that I'm not riding that quickly but it's not long before I'm entering the final five star secteur at Carrefour de l'Arbre. Halfway through the secteur I'm riding in the left hand gutter and can see the famous Café in the distance as I register somebody riding toward me. My first thought is what the hell is he doing, he's going the wrong way! As he gets closer I can hear him screaming at me in a foreign language which sounds like Italian. Now he raises one hand from the bars and begins gesticulating for me to get out of his way. Bloody foreigners on fucking mountain bikes! I reluctantly leave my smooth line giving way to him, if we were in Blighty I might not have been so forgiving. I pass the café leaving the pave turning right onto the main road before taking an immediate left onto the penultimate secteur.

Even though these last two secteurs are fairly easy I'm not taking any chances at this late stage which is reflected in my meticulously careful choice of riding line. As I finally leave the pave behind me for a second time I catch the wheel of another lone rider. He might be Russian as he's wearing a Katusha team jersey but then again he could be from anywhere given the global appeal of this race, I think I've spoken to or seen someone from every continent on the planet. Without exchanging a word we give each other a knowing look and I go to the front putting the hammer down. After a couple of hundred metres he comes past and takes his turn on the front whilst I catch my breath in his slipstream. Sitting on his wheel I take the opportunity to drain my last water bottle and do something I've always wanted to do. I know it's not very environmentally friendly but hoping to look extremely professional I throw the empty bottle at the opposite pavement. We carry on powering towards Roubaix in our two up time trial taking equal turns not speaking just enjoying the sensation of being able to generate so much speed after a long hard day in the saddle.

As we reach the main boulevard leading back to the velodrome I swing off and relax not wanting to negotiate the heavy Saturday afternoon traffic at speed as my partner disappears into the distance immediately running a red light. I observe the traffic regulations, no point being reckless after all the hard work to get here. My little white car looms into view, as I pass I give it a quick once over, Roubaix isn't the most salubrious of places after all. The first right turn takes me onto the Rue Alexandre Fleming, being careful to avoid the potholes I make the second right turn through the iron gates into the most famous velodrome in the world. Again, as last year I saviour every pedal stroke round the final bend to the finish giving a Winston Churchillesque two finger V for victory salute as I cross the line.

Two Challenges down, one to go.

'It never gets easier, you just get faster'
Greg Lemond (the only American winner of the Tour de France 1986, '89 & '90)

Strava data for Paris Roubaix Challenge 2016-
Distance	105.3 miles
Moving time	7 hours 2 minutes
Average speed	14.9mph
Elevation gain	1782ft

The second Challenge generated a further £95 of donations bringing the grand total raised so far to £1,460.00

This is a selection of well wishes from our supporters-

'Amazing ride well done Ritchie.'

'Well done Ritchie all shake rattle and roll, hope you get a good nights sleep you deserve it. Hope the aches and pains aren't too bad, thank you for everything you are doing.'

'Do you not feel a bit like a pilgrim making it to the Holy ground? If you don't well I feel it for you.'

Straight Outta Compton

'When my legs hurt I say "Shut up legs!" '
Jens Voight (former professional cyclist)

Fuck me it's hot!

To make matters worse I've got earache from having to listen to Mr Bigshot regale us with tales of how big his biggest bottle of champagne is, obviously a penis extension. My wife Chriss and I are sat in the scorched garden of the Veuve Clicquot champagne house in Reims, (pronounced like phlegm) France with two other couples drinking fizz after taking a tour of the maze like underground cellars where millions of pounds of grape juice are stored.

For some reason wherever I go I always seem to find myself in the company of that one most annoying arsehole who not only loves the sound of his own voice but happens to be a complete know it all. Any experience you may have had you can guarantee he's done it but only bigger and better with brass knobs on.

His, young enough to be daughter, partner in her ever so posh Home Counties accent asks my wife if Veuve is her favourite champagne. I almost choke on my fizz at her reaction to my wife's response of 'I'm not bothered as long as it's got bubbles', anyone would think Chriss had just told her to go pleasure herself. To add insult to injury Chriss continues by telling her how I don't even like champagne and only drink beer. What heathens.

For the third and final Challenge, partly due to logistical reasons but also because I wanted Chriss to experience first-hand the atmosphere at one of the rides, we have decided to take a road trip and have stopped en route to the Alps in the heart of champagne country.

After surviving a second 'hell of the north' in as many years I have the best part of three months to prepare for the final Challenge which means I have lots of time to get plenty of miles in and thus increase my stamina base. Unfortunately my training tends to be mostly on flat roads given my geographical location and I'm constantly aware that due to circumstance I'm neglecting the necessary climbing training I'll require for L'Etape. This prompts me to seek a suitable sportive which will test my climbing skills or perhaps lack of them beforehand.

Nowadays it's possible, if you so desire, to participate in a sportive almost every weekend throughout the year such are the proliferation of events. However I need to find an event that is suitable in that it is firstly a similar distance to L'Etape, secondly it must involve a decent amount of climbing, thirdly it needs to be within the final weeks before the Challenge and lastly it has to be relatively close to home. And, of course it also needs to fit in with my dogs, work and commitments at home. After much searching I finally manage to find an event which fulfils many of my criteria, albeit a little earlier than would be ideal. The Roman Road Challenge a circular route starting and finishing at Edge Hill University in western Lancashire held on the 29th May at just over 83 miles involving 4200 feet of climbing should prove itself to be a good test.

What isn't particularly good is my preparation leading up to the event. As with the majority of sportives the Roman Road Challenge is held on a Sunday, I finish working nights that Saturday morning the day before so I'm already feeling quite fatigued. To make my preparation even worse the lads from work are having a traditionally British 'all dayer' in Blackpool as a mini stag do for a colleague. Despite much ridicule I make my excuses in the early evening and leave the party in full swing already feeling a little the worse for wear.

The next morning I get up as late as possible and make the hour long journey to Edge Hill eating my standard pre sportive breakfast of bananas and energy bars in the car on the way there. By the time I've signed on and sorted myself out I'm in the very last group of about thirty riders to start, maybe this explains the fast pace we make through the country lanes on the outskirts of Ormskirk. I hide in the wheels saving energy whilst attempting to clear my head from the effects of sleep deprivation and alcohol. No wonder the roads look very familiar to me, the route passes Blythe Hall once the home of playwright and socialite Noel Coward where Chriss and I were married several years ago.

The first test of Hunters Hill comes soon after where I find myself surprisingly going pretty well passing many other riders on the climb. The route meanders heading east past Chorley through Horwich taking in a sharp steep climb over Rivington Pike onto the moors above Bolton, where I again leave numerous riders in my wake, then undulates towards Blackburn on the old roman road hence the name of the event. Up down, up down, short steep climbs sapping the strength from my legs. I've been riding alone for some time now so have been having to do all the work myself which means I'm feeling rather tired when the route starts heading back westwards towards Preston. I know these roads very well as I've ridden them many times over the years. I'm caught by another rider and manage to stay on his wheel getting a tow for several miles. Wheel sucking is considered poor etiquette in cycling but I simply don't have the 'legs' to take a turn on the front. A small train of fast riders comes past us heading back towards Ormskirk with my companion managing to make the effort to join them which once again leaves me suffering by myself for the last few miles to the finish.

I eventually finish 58th out of a field 236 strong, covering 83.3 miles with a time of exactly 5 hours 13 minutes placing me just inside the top twenty five percent, not bad for an old fat lad given the circumstances.

To improve your performance it's necessary to reflect and objectively analyse your previous efforts. The more I consider my last outing at the Roman Road Challenge the more I become concerned that the reason for me feeling so tired that day towards the latter third of the ride was due to the effects of the climbs and not necessarily the poor preparation.

Success is as much mental as it is physical, just ask Dr Steve Peters sports psychologist to the stars and former member of *British Cycling* senior management team who helped create the most successful Olympic cycling team in the history of the sport, known as 'the medal factory' or any of his high profile clients such as snooker genius Ronnie O'Sullivan, I'm sure they'll all agree.

My final preparation for the third Challenge comes exactly a week before L'Etape being a sportive named *White Roads Classic* which is organised by a group called 'Cycle Classics' whose modus operandi is to create events that have been inspired by the Classics, hence *Tour of the Black Country* (Paris Roubaix) and *Cheshire Cobbled Classic* (Tour of Flanders) being amongst the other main events they run. Having ridden a couple of their events in the past I'm expecting this to also be a rigorous test, I still have painful memories of the suffer fest that is the *Cheshire Cobbled Classic.*

The inspiration for the *White Roads Classic* has come from a semi classic held in early March in the area of Tuscany, Italy called *Strade Bianche* which features the historic white gravel roads of the region and culturally stunning finish in Siena that have come to epitomise the race. Despite only being on the professional calendar since 2007 word around the campfire is that the race is already held in such high regard that it will eventually become the sixth *Monument*. However the race was actually inspired by an amateur event called L'Eroica which pays homage to a bygone era of cycling with participants being allowed to only use bicycles and equipment that was available before 1980.

As much as I'd like to ride Strade Bianche the logistical nightmare of getting over to Tuscany means it's unlikely I shall ever add it to my palmares and will therefore have to settle for 'Cycle Classics' own 128 kilometre version featuring 18 sectors of gravel and chalk roads centred around the historic area of The Ridgeway in Oxfordshire. Think of the iconic Iron Age white horse cut into the hillside and you're in the right postcode.

The beauty of the summer's morning is matched by that of the start venue of Basildon Park, used in the filming of Downton Abbey, a few miles from the town of Reading. As I'm one of the earliest arrivals I find myself in the first group to start the event which quickly reaches a pace I find uncomfortable and I begin to drift to the back of the small peloton. I may have mentioned before but I like a few miles to warm up the lungs and muscles to settle into a nice rhythm. In cycling these are referred to as your engine and should you compare this to a vehicle it's known as having mechanical sympathy.

Before too long we encounter the first sector and despite being a veteran of Flanders and Roubaix I'm unpleasantly surprised by the roughness of the so called white road. The advertising spiel for the event on the website states that the sectors *'have been selected as suitable for road bikes.'* Well I'm sorry but I have to disagree due to the numerous boulders ranging from golf ball to football size which would make riding a mountain bike over them even uncomfortable. After the second equally hardcore sector I'm passing through the village of Compton when my front wheel goes instantly flat with a loud and ominous bang. As I reinflate the tyre having changed the inner tube I notice the sidewall of the tyre has split and the more air I pump in the more the black rubber bulges through the shredded wall in a strained effort to escape.

That's it, race over. I guess Strade Bianche isn't meant to be.

There's a silver lining to every cloud though, which in this case is that at least I didn't suffer this mishap during either of my first two Challenges where I was using the very same tyres.

The more I ponder over the final Challenge the more concerned I become. I begin to think that maybe I've bitten off more than I can chew, I know the distance won't prove to be a problem but four high mountain passes could well be a leg breaker. Years ago when my annual summer holiday was a week following the Tour de France the most 'Cols' I ever climbed in a single day was when we rode out of Briancon over the Col de Montgenevre into Italy finishing at the summit of Sestriere. But, like I say that was years ago. From researching the route of L'Etape I'm aware that the last two climbs of the day the Col des Aravis and Col de Joux Plane are considered to be extremely difficult. This isn't to say that the other climbs will be easy because from experience I can guarantee they won't be, in the Alps they are all hard it's just varying degrees of difficulty.

Confidence is a big factor in being successful and I can feel mine slowly ebbing away.

Fate, karma, call it what you will but there's a reason that I believe more often than not that 'things' have a way of working out. Less than a month before L'Etape I'm browsing the internet when I come across a tweet posted by two time Tour winner Chris Froome. There's a picture of him and fellow Team Sky rider Geraint Thomas during a reconnaissance ride of stage 20, the stage being used for L'Etape, which shows a huge rock landslide completely blocking the road on the Col de la Ramaz. Upon further investigation there has been a very recent announcement by the organisers of the event that for safety reasons the route of L'Etape has had to be altered and will now no longer include the Col de la Ramaz.

You fucking dancer!

The revised route excluding the Col de la Ramaz will now be twelve kilometres shorter but more importantly *only* include three catergorised high mountain passes.

Now I'm back in the game.

It is worth noting to put my effort into perspective that Stage 20 of the Tour de France was run in its complete entirety being won by Jon Izaguirre of Spain in a time of 4 hours 6 minutes 45 seconds.

And the weather was atrocious.

It Ain't Half Hot Mum

'Pain is temporary, it may last a minute, or an hour, or a day, or a year but eventually it will subside and something else will take its place. If I quit however it lasts forever.'
Lance Armstrong (disgraced former pro serving lifetime ban for systematic doping programme)

After spending a couple of days playing tourists in Reims we continue with the second part of the road trip making the six hour drive south into the French Alps. When we reach our final destination of Sallanches on Friday afternoon, a few miles north of Megeve where the race will start, our first impressions are of how hot it is. It was hot in Reims but this seems far hotter, more intense. We are staying in a traditional alpine wood cabin which during winter with a roaring log fire is no doubt blissfully toasty. However in the height of summer it's stinking fucking hot, uncomfortably so which means neither of us sleeps particularly well that night.

The next day we make the short drive climbing out of Sallanches into the centre of Megeve where we turn left and head even further up the mountain to the altiport at Cote 2000 where the L'Etape Village is situated to sign on. Tomorrow the race will actually start down in the town opposite the cemetery on the Route Nationale. Both Chriss and I are surprised at the number of cyclists riding up the mountain to sign on, me I'm saving my legs for tomorrow thank you very much. The views are absolutely breathtaking, Mont Blanc wearing a cloak of pristine white snow dominating the mountainous skyline.

It is without hyperbole that the signing on area has been called a Village for it literally is a small village. Most sportives will have a few merchandising stalls with mechanics and fast food sellers on site but none of them are on the grandiose scale of L'Etape. The Village easily covers an area of at least two acres, there must be over two hundred stalls selling all manner of cycling related merchandise with all the major bicycle manufacturers displaying their latest models.

This is a cycling pervert idea of bike porn heaven. There are doctors, mechanics and masseuses available, entertainment areas for the kids, numerous food stalls as well a huge TV screen to watch the day's action from Le Tour. You could easily spend several hours here and probably not experience all it has to offer. It also serves to reinforce the magnitude and scale of this event.

The rest of the day is spent attempting to stay hydrated, carbo loading, checking then re-checking all my equipment whilst trying to rest as much as possible following the cyclists mantra:

Why stand when you can sit, why sit when you can lie down.
Besides it is far too bloody hot to do anything.

Sunday 10th July 2016

After another restless night due to the stifling heat my alarm goes off. The first thing I'm aware of is how hot it already is, in fact you can't fail to notice the heat. Despite the forecast of thunderstorms there's not a cloud in the sky, worryingly it looks set to be another scorcher.

Yesterday the journey to Megeve only took us twenty minutes, however today due to event traffic it takes the best part of three quarters of an hour. Again we're amazed at the number of cyclists riding to the start. On the outskirts of town we're directed by an event marshal into the 'Kiss and Ride' area where relatives can drop off participants, located in the carpark of the local Casino supermarche and told in no uncertain terms we are allowed just ten minutes to unload. I hurriedly ready my bike, cramming gels and energy bars into my pockets before kissing my wife goodbye. As I slowly pedal away she shouts after me 'Good Luck!'

Unlike the other two Challenges which featured open starts L'Etape has for safety and logistical reasons very strict starting protocols. The start area on the main road through Megeve is completely and securely sectioned off, consisting of sixteen pens each with the capacity of holding a thousand riders. Rider numbers have been assigned according to information supplied during the registration process according to experience, ability and previous results submitted. From the start line to the back of the last pen is a distance of over a mile. Participants have been informed to make their way to the designated pen an hour before their start time, that each pen will close fifteen minutes prior to the allocated start time and if you're late you will be relegated to the next pen. Once inside the pen you will not be permitted to leave for any reason, even a nervous piss. The whole process is run with military precision.

My race number is 9374 allotted to pen #9 with a start time of 08:07:30

As I enter the pen I've been assigned to, again wearing my Team British Cycling jersey which I've worn during the other two Challenges, I'm almost accosted by a fellow Brit who seems desperate to engage somebody in conversation. He appears quite nervous which I can empathise with not to mention hot with his full beard and is rather rotund for a cyclist, however I've learnt not to judge a book by its cover. We discuss our preparation for the event and to be honest it doesn't sound like he's done an awful lot which is even more surprising when he tells me how he participated in last year's L'Etape but was caught by the broom wagon and eliminated. The broom wagon is a vehicle which follows the race *sweeping up* riders who are unable to finish within an allotted time. He goes on to tell me how he's travelled here from England with his father by train to Lyon then rented a hire car which he's dumped *somewhere* nearby leaving his father back at their hotel. I ask him how he plans to get back here to pick up the car from the finish in Morzine. His answer of 'I'll cross that bridge when I come to it' completely astonishes me. I really don't understand how people can arrive so unprepared, this isn't the sort of event you can have any hope of finishing by winging it. I took part in another sportive where I was getting ready and happened to overhear the bloke in the car next to mine say to his companion that he'd forgotten his cycling shoes.

Piss poor preparation leads to piss poor performance.

As the pens in front of us empty one by one we are instructed to move forward shuffling along like two wheeled convicts eventually reaching the start line. A voice comes over a loudspeaker first speaking in French then English telling us we are about to undertake an amazing challenge and to enjoy a safe ride. Impressively at just after the allocated time as stated in the handbook I roll across the start line beginning my third and final Challenge. I don't see the bloke I'd been chatting with ever again and will never know whether he finished or even made it back to his car. The route starts quickly as it's all downhill leaving Megeve in a south easterly direction towards the town of Flumet. This is disconcerting as what goes up must come down and vice versa.

Sure enough the road soon starts to go uphill, riders ahead of me as far as I can see are gaining height above my position. The peloton appears to be a living entity, snaking round the hairpin bends like a huge colourful human centipede. This isn't the first mountain of the day though, oh no this isn't even a categorised climb this is just a precursor to soften up the legs.

A short but technical descent leads us down into the town of Flumet then through onto the beginning of the first categorised climb of the Col des Aravis, rated a 2nd Cat at 5.4 miles in length with an average gradient of 6% gaining 1653 feet of elevation. The climb begins gently enough as I casually spin the pedals keeping a high cadence hoping to prevent the build-up of lactic acid in my legs. We soon emerge from the wooded lower slopes into alpine pastures taking in the stunning mountain views as we climb ever higher and higher rounding the switchbacks to the sound of cattle bells.

It's a beautiful day, already becoming very warm despite the early hour. After about forty five minutes of steady climbing the summit comes into view, I've purposely been taking it easy at this early juncture. I pull over at the summit at an altitude of 1498 metres so I can stretch my muscles off, take on board some refreshments and capture the obligatory picture of the summit sign. Upon checking my phone I find a good luck tweet off Susie Dent from Countdowns dictionary corner. Nice one Suze.

It strikes me that there is some kind of strange celebrity coincidence happening during my Challenge. First of all I shared a coach with Martin Johnson at Roubaix, we have received donations from Rachel Riley and Suzie Dent of Countdown and only yesterday Amy Williams MBE Olympic gold medallist in the Skeleton posted on *Instagram* that she was taking part in L'Etape. What I discover some time later is that she is participating with several other celebrities of varying cycling ability in the making of a reality television show called *Tour de Celeb* due to be aired on Channel5 in the autumn. I'm sure you'll be able to find it somewhere on the internet as it's well worth a watch.

My plan is to take it easy on the climbs whilst trying to make up time on the descents then use other riders to tow me along through the valleys between the mountains. I've always been quite adept at descending and anyone who has ridden a high mountain pass will know full well the exhilaration of a high speed descent. However when there's thousands of other riders, none of whom you've ever ridden with before, all vying for the same bit of road it becomes prudent to be cautious rather than going balls out. I take it steady letting the speed build gradually, allowing gravity to take effect, concentrating on my lines through the hairpins braking smoothly into the corners then accelerating away, all the while trying to maintain a safety zone around myself. All too soon the thrill is over as the road begins to level out and I have to start pedalling again to maintain my momentum. The temperature has noticeably increased once back down in the valley.

You'd imagine at an event with so many participants that it would be easy to latch onto a wheel yet riders are strewn all over the road in dribs and drabs, some I catch are going slower than me or conversely going quicker which means I end up doing most of the work myself. Pacing is essential in any sportive but it's of paramount importance today in this heat faced with such mountainous terrain.

It's getting increasingly hotter by the minute.

It's not long before the second categorised climb of the day starts, the 1st Cat Col de la Colombiere. I've covered just twenty three miles in an hour and three quarters. The Colombiere is 7.2 miles long at an average gradient of 6% gaining 2167 feet in elevation. I drop onto the small chainring settling into a steady rhythm constantly checking the heartrate monitor on my wrist trying to keep it beneath 150 beats per minute, any higher than this and I'll be entering the upper limits of my aerobic threshold.

Heart rate monitors are a valuable training aid which can effectively help gauge the maximum effort you are able to maintain before the body is overcome by lactate acid leading to exhaustion. Sports science has come on leaps and bounds since the good old bad old days of simply training to a point of complete fatigue and the idea of nutrition being a steak dinner before a race. One of the most talented riders to ever turn a pedal in anger Fausto Coppi was advised by his doctor to smoke three cigarettes a day to help increase his heart rate. Can you imagine being given that kind of advice today by a medical professional. Whole books have been written on the subject but to put it in layman terms your maximum heart rate is 220 minus your age, then 'training zones' can be calculated as a percentage of this figure. Unless you're incredibly fit a training zone above 80% of your maximum heart rate for a sustained period of time can be difficult to achieve. Chris Boardman former Olympic pursuit champion, World Hour record holder and one of the most underrated cyclists of his generation in my opinion swore by them. However the fashion of the day has now moved towards the use of power meters which measure how many watts of power you are producing at any given time indicating the amount of effort being exerted.

    This climb is very aesthetically pleasing and similar in gradient to the Aravis, which means I am able to tap out a decent pace without going into the red, but at over two and a half miles longer means by the time I reach the summit at 1618 metres above sea level after just over an hour of climbing I'm pissing sweat and my legs are beginning to complain. Again I take a quick time out at the summit following the regimen I'd decided upon before starting the race. A group of about ten Japanese riders dressed in Rapha clothing arrive at the summit all riding high end bicycles, there must be a hundred grands worth of gear just there. They look extremely happy to be taking part and in the stereotypical fashion of Japanese tourists whip out their cameras for selfies and group photos.

    I remount my bike beginning the descent leaving them to their impromptu photo session. As the speed builds quickly I take in the beautiful scenery acutely aware of the precipitous drop immediately to my right awaiting me should I suffer a lapse of concentration. It really is a fabulous descent made all the more reassuring knowing the roads are closed and that you're not going to encounter a camper van head on rounding one of the many hairpin bends which has happened to me on more than one occasion during previous rides in the mountains. I'm flying along an unusually long straight section before heading into a fast sweeping left hand bend and as I exit the corner there's a marshal in the road indicating for riders to slow down. Gently squeezing the brakes I can see an ambulance ahead with blue lights flashing parked on the left hand side of the road as another rider flies past brakes squealing loudly in protest then a bang as his tyre explodes due to the build-up of heat and pressure. Crawling past the ambulance out of the corner of my eye I catch a glimpse of a prone rider curled up in a foetal position being attended to by a paramedic. It looks like somebody has spilt a carafe of red wine on the road next to him. Fuck's sake. I can only assume he's taken the bend too fast lost control and collided with the wall. For the remainder of the descent I keep the speed in check attempting to steer clear of other riders in my path.

Back on the relative safety of the valley roads I immediately notice how hot it is and again find myself isolated. It doesn't surprise me in the slightest when I pass a chemist where the green illuminated neon sign gives the temperature as 35 degrees. Could be worse, it could be pissing down. I soon catch a French couple enjoying the slipstream effect as much as the view of the woman's tanned shapely calves but after a mile or so find their pace to be too conservative for my liking so strike out on my own. Not long after I start to rue my decision as the effort starts to tell on my legs.

It's turning into something of a slog through the valley but silver lining to every cloud at least I'm not having to drag my fat arse up the climb of the Ramaz. After a few miles a decent sized group passes me so I make the effort to join them but it doesn't take me long to realise they're going at a pace which I soon find uncomfortable and I begin to blow like a barn door in a storm. Just as a small gap starts to appear between myself and the rider in front another guy jumps past me and takes the wheel filling the gap much to my relief. An English girl looking much fresher than myself draws alongside remarking on how that bloke had just stolen my wheel. Giving her a cheeky Colgate smile I say 'He's welcome to it, I just hope you haven't been sat there sucking my wheel checking out my arse?' She laughs at the ridiculousness of my suggestion and as we chat I feel the pace increasing which again causes a small gap to appear. I gesture for her to take the wheel which she seems to do with relative ease leaving me to watch as the group slowly disappears up the road out of sight. Once more I'm left in no man's land.

More worryingly though is I'm starting to feel a bit of cramp in my right vastus medialis, the muscle above the inside of the knee. I'm guessing the cramp is a result of dehydration, despite trying to drink as much as possible my body just isn't accustomed to dealing with this kind of heat. Well that's my excuse anyway and I'm sticking to it. In an attempt to stave off dehydration prior to the event I'd fitted to my bike a pair of rear mounted bottle cages attached to the rails of the saddle as used specifically by triathletes which means I can carry two extra bidons. The only drawback to this is that it means I'm carrying an extra few kilos but given that at my last weigh in I tip the scales at just over eighty kilograms it's an acceptable handicap.

The final feed zone is situated in the town of Samoens strategically placed just prior to the final climb of the day the Joux Plane so I pull in to stretch my legs off and refill my bottles in preparation for the hardest part of the race. As I unclip from the pedals my right thigh is suddenly gripped by a spasm of cramp. The pain is excruciating, all I can do is lean over the handlebars in agony gritting my teeth waiting for the spasm to subside hoping nobody has noticed my distress. Eventually the muscles unlock enough for me to swing my leg over the top tube which only serves to cause an aftershock of cramp this one thankfully less debilitating than the first. I hobble across the courtyard to a shaded quiet corner and manage to sit down my weary muscles protesting at the effort.

Whilst I give my legs time to recover I cram the last of my energy bars down my neck. A few painful stretches and a quick massage to the affected areas and I feel almost ready to crack on. All I have to do is get up the Joux Plane then its downhill all the way to the finish, surely I can manage that.

Passing underneath the banner signalling the beginning of the final climb I find out how steep the Joux Plane actually is, it is literally like hitting a wall. Any momentum I had is lost immediately as I engage the smallest gear I have even struggling to turn that one over. Somebody moves past me shouting 'This is the steepest part it gets easier after this!' I shout after him 'Thank fuck for that!'

Myself and the other competitors continue our gurning contest as we struggle up the viciously vertiginous incline. I don't even bother looking at my heart rate monitor as I can tell I'm already deep into the red, barely able to turn the pedals over I'm almost down to walking pace. At least I'm not alone in my suffering, everyone else seems to be having as hard a time of it as I am, in fact a great number of riders have already dismounted and are either slowly walking or seeking shade from the relentless heat under the trees. I'm determined not to get off besides I think if I do that'll be it, game over.

Despite going so slowly I'm passing literally hundreds of competitors who appear to be having even a harder time than I am. Every kilometre there are road markers which tell you how far you have left to go to the summit and the average gradient of the next kilometre, I slowly tick them off one by one. As I'm taking a drink a very fit looking forty something French lady, fit as in athletic not Rachel Riley fit, appears at my side and gestures to my bidon in a drinking motion. I pass her the bottle and to my astonishment she takes a gulp any self-respecting pisshead would be proud of almost draining it. With a curt 'Merci' she pedals effortlessly away. Merci indeed.

Have I mentioned how hot it is? The only other time I've experienced heat like this is the first time I rode Mont Ventoux all those years ago. The sweat is literally pissing out of me, any attempts to stay hydrated have gone out the window. I know this because I can feel the cramp in my thighs lurking in the background waiting to strike with a vice like grip at any moment. I grit my teeth and grind the pedals over hoping I've got enough left in the tank to make it to the far off summit which makes me think of the song 'Top of the Mountain' by one of my favourite artists Paul Weller;

'At the foot of the mountain
Such a long way to climb
How will I ever get up there,
Though I know I must try'

The Joux Plane is certainly living up to its fearsome reputation.

Unless you have ridden a high mountain pass in the Alps it's difficult to articulate how incredibly hard these climbs are, even those with easier ratings are still much more demanding physically than anything you will find in Britain. These climbs go on for mile after mile the gradients slowly sapping the strength from your legs, the only reprieve coming on the hairpin bends where the corners flatten albeit briefly. And then there's the heat of high summer to deal with.

Approaching a right hand bend I notice another ambulance, there are several people under the shade of a tree gathered round a prone cyclist. His legs are covered with a space blanket like those given to runners finishing the London marathon, and fuck me I hope I'm mistaken but it looks like they're performing CPR. This is *not* good.

After an hour and a half of relentless leg destroying climbing I pass the last road marker indicating the final kilometre of the climb, thank fuck for that as I'm on the rivet. Being 'on the rivet' is perhaps one of the oldest sayings in cycling meaning you are at your maximum threshold and unable to go any deeper. Its origin comes from the old fashion cycling saddles which were made from leather and used rivets to attach the material to the shell with the ones on the nose of the saddle visible to the eye. A rider under stress would sit right on the very nose of the saddle in an attempt to generate as much power as possible hence the phrase 'on the rivet' being coined. Not long after I slowly come to a stop as I eventually pass under the banner at the summit, a sharp stabbing wave of cramp hitting my thighs as I unclip from the pedals. Head hanging over the handlebars I breathe slowly and deeply trying to get my shit together waiting for the pain to dissipate. Unlike when I stopped at the summit of the other two mountains this time very few riders come past me. An English lad young enough to be my son stops to tell me that I look how he feels, he also mentions that he had to stop and walk some of the climb. I take weary pride in letting him know that I never stopped.

Almost ten minutes must have passed before I summon the effort to carry on freewheeling along the slight descent away from the summit. The views of the mountains to my left are absolutely stunning whilst on my right is the most invitingly beautiful alpine lake. I consider stopping to take a dip in the crystal clear water but don't fancy a wet, cold descent to the finish so I carry on gliding along enjoying the incredible views. However there's a rather nasty and unwelcome sting in the tail as the road starts to climb again for a few hundred metres to the summit of the Col du Ranfolly, talk about adding insult to injury, after which six miles of twisting and fairly technical descent will take me to the finish in Morzine.

I take it pretty steady on the descent partly because I don't want to come a cropper when I'm so close to finishing the Challenge but also due to being so fatigued I don't want to lose concentration and end up going arse over tit. Also some of the things I've seen today have reaffirmed to me that this is supposed to be *fun*. I'm almost at the bottom of the descent approaching a right hand hairpin when the rider I've been following seems to make no attempt to turn for the corner carrying straight on off the road somersaulting over the edge into the field. When you're following somebody's wheel its easy, especially when you're tired, to engage auto-pilot which means I only just make the corner watching the incident unfold in front of me in slow motion. I laugh giddily at his misfortune relieved to have stayed upright leading me to recall a similar moment from the 2003 Tour when on a mountain descent to the stage finish in Gap one of Armstrong's main rivals Joseba Beloki had a nasty crash breaking his hip and effectively ending his career. Showing remarkable cool not to mention exceptional bike handling skills Armstrong swerved round the prone rider off the road crossing a ploughed field before rejoining the course. The final kilometre of the race seems familiar to me from previous Tour stages that have finished in Morzine that I have watched on the television. Approaching the finish I feel a range of emotions, pride and satisfaction at having completed the Challenge as well as a sense of relief at having survived the gruelling experience unscathed.

Several years ago I used to frequent a bike shop in Leyland owned by an ex professional called Bill Nickson who had ridden the Tour in 1977. During one visit I asked him what the experience had been like and his answer of 'It was all a blur really' puzzled me at the time. I now know what he meant.

Crossing the line I hear a familiar voice from behind the barriers to my left shout out my name. Pulling over I gingerly unclip feeling a stab of cramp in my thigh and give my wife a massive hug. I did it! As Chriss negotiates the barriers I'm handed my well earnt finishers medal. We slowly make our way down to the post ride area where I gladly park my bike and make my way down the bank of the Dranse river. Several other competitors have also had the idea of cooling off in the refreshingly cool alpine water. By the time Chriss returns from the bar I'm submerged in the crystal clear water up to my waist hoping the cold water will ease the cramps. That beer so hard earned, never tasted so good. Cheers.

Would I have completed the Challenge had the route not been altered? Honestly, probably not because it was a beautifully tough course and I was proven right to be as worried and nervous as I was beforehand. By the finish I was totally cooked and it may well have been a case of a mountain too far. But it's a moot point now anyway.

Strava data for L'Etape du Tour 2016-
Distance   77.4 miles
Moving time   6 hours 37 minutes
Average speed   11.7mph
Elevation gain   11,447ft

The third and final Challenge generated a further £260 of donations bringing the grand total raised to £2,050.00

A few words from our supporters-

'Fantastic………just had a look at your pics, looked hard work in all that heat! Well done again X'
'Many congratulations. Along your long journey you have raised awareness of the cruel and unnecessary treatment of these beautiful dogs that are willing to forgive us for the evil inflicted on them.'
'Well done Ritchie, you are a star and a hero for all the doggies that you have helped. X'

Donation Donation Donation

'Riding bicycles will not only benefit the individual doing it, but the world at large.'
Udo E. Simonis (Professor of Environmental Science)

There's an old girl who lives round the corner from us called Mavis who I see frequently as I usually pass her house at least once a day whilst out walking the dogs. Despite being a late octogenarian she is in full control of her faculties and enjoys making a fuss of the dogs regularly buying them treats. On one such occasion as I was passing her house she came out to greet us, surreptitiously thrusting a plain white envelope into my hand. What she said was to prove very profound and resonate throughout the Challenge.

'I know how difficult it is to fundraise' she tells me knowingly.

As she pets the dogs she relives the story of how her husband died some twenty years ago of cancer which prompted her to undertake several fundraising ventures on behalf of Cancer Research. Inside the envelope was a crisp ten pound note.

The first person to make a donation is one of my wife's close friends, Colette. My wife, in stark contrast to myself, has many friends but Colette is from the inner sanctum of friends known by all of us as 'the Spain Eight', think *The Golden Girls* but times eight and twenty years before they were golden. Colette also left us a message, *'We aren't doggy people but we are Greenwood people!'*

For me those words from Colette epitomised the ideology I was hoping would be the reaction to my Challenge. Whether you're a doggy person or not, whether you like cycling or not I expected my family and friends to support what I considered to be a fairly worthy and momentous undertaking. However sadly this was not the case and I certainly found out who my real friends were, as well as coming to the realisation that people do not appreciate being asked for money.

There were a handful of people that I had known for many years who I considered to be friends and at some stage in our lives had had quite a close relationship with that simply refused point blank to donate. To say I was disappointed is an understatement and I had no qualms in immediately discontinuing those friendships. Their names have no place in my book as it is my intention to treat them with the disdain they deserve. Then there are those people who kept promising to donate but failed to do so and the ones who thought that by ignoring your requests you'd go away.

One person refused to donate claiming she didn't like dogs, cats, donkeys or animals in general for that matter. I'm very suspicious of people who demonstrate a lack of respect and empathy for nature and the other creatures that inhabit this planet. I think it confirms the arrogance of human beings that we believe we can do whatever we want to this planet without repercussion.

'What have they done to the Earth?
What have they done to our fair sister?
Ravaged and plundered and ripped her and bit her.
Stuck her with knives in the side of the dawn, and tied her with fences and dragged her down.'
James Douglas Morrison (Poet and Lead singer of The Doors)

Only the other day I was out cycling on one of my regular routes when I had to stop to negotiate a five bar gate blocking a now disused lane between farmers' fields. In the adjacent field was an all-terrain type vehicle with the words **LANCASHIRE MOLE CONTROL** written on the side and a bloke in combat fatigues taking his morning brew from a thermos flask. Already knowing what his answer will be I shout across to him 'So what happens to the moles?' with an oddly satisfying smirk he replies 'They're killed.'

'Shame that doesn't happens to some humans!' I shout back and leave him to ponder this profound observation as I pedal away.

Within a number of days we have smashed our initial target of one hundred pounds and promptly raise the bar to a massive one thousand pounds.

Quite quickly the fundraising becomes rather addictive as my wife has created an email account which receives notifications from the donation webpage letting us know when somebody has made a contribution. As we seem to be in receipt of donations on an almost daily basis every time my phone goes I feel a sense of nervous excitement in anticipation of anther generous benefactor helping us towards our target. Whether it's a fiver, ten quid or more the amount really isn't significant, the fact that people are willing to support us and raising awareness for the animals is what counts. However every time my phone goes and we haven't received a donation I can't help but feel somewhat deflated and disappointed.

What astonishes us most is the number of complete and total strangers who are willing to donate. I guess this just goes to prove the power of social media and that all my wife's efforts in putting together our Challenge pages has been time well spent. Also the dog world is rather an insular place which means that by networking we are able to cast our net far and wide. Don't get me wrong this is no easy task during which both my wife and I spend considerable time in an attempt to raise the profile of the Challenge and draw attention to the plight of these unfortunate animals.

For me the highlight of the whole fundraising experience comes in late March as we're well on our way to reaching our amended target of a thousand pounds. I'm sat at the computer networking on social media when I see that Suzie Dent of Countdowns dictionary corner has tweeted about a charity bike ride her and fellow co-host Rachel Riley are taking part in at the end of May called 'Ride the Night' in support of women against cancer.

When I met my wife she found it amusing that I had Countdown on a series link and was taken aback when I told her that I'd been watching the show since the very beginning and had always held aspirations of becoming a contestant. My wife proved to be the catalyst in me having my fifteen minutes of fame as she pressured me into submitting my application. That's how I came to find myself at Media City in Salford Quays feeling almost as nervous as the day I got married as I was about to fulfil a lifelong ambition and one that would be available for the world and his wife to see, well sixty million Brits at least should they so desire. I keep repeating the words to myself 'Whatever you do don't embarrass yourself!' I was fortunate enough to sit in the *Champions chair* on two occasions but was defeated at my third appearance which actually came as something of a relief due to the mounting pressure. Although the programme is aired on a daily basis they film in advance up to five shows a day which meant my brain was absolutely frazzled by the end of recording the third show. However I wasn't beaten by any old schmuck, oh no the contestant who got the better of me only went on to win the whole darn series. I have to say that day of filming as a contestant on Countdown was one of the best experiences I've ever enjoyed, it really was a fantastic day and the people behind the show were remarkably accommodating hosts to their credit. Besides which I got to meet the other love of my life Rachel Riley and let me tell you with all sincerity she is even more beautiful in the flesh not to mention being a thoroughly lovely person, vegan and committed animal rights activist. For the uninitiated, winning contestants receive the now legendary teapot which has pride of place on our kitchen windowsill. My wife always asks me why I couldn't have gone on a gameshow where the winner's prize was a substantial amount of cash and not a useless piece of crockery.

When I was growing up I was always told that if you didn't ask you didn't get and I've always been a cheeky chappy so I respond to Suzie Dents tweet by reminding her I'd been a contestant on the show, informing her of my own charity cycling Challenge and suggesting she might want to help raise its profile by using her celebrity status. Within five minutes my phone goes 'Ping'. She's only gone and donated ten quid! I can't quite believe it and in my giddy excitement decide I might as well be in for a penny as in for a pound so send a tweet to Rachel telling her what has happened encouraging her not to be left out. Again, a few minutes later there's another ping from my phone. The notification says '**Rachel Riley has donated £10**'. I'm completely and utterly gobsmacked. Rachel you beauty!

For me this is the absolute pinnacle of the whole fundraiser and if we don't receive another single penny I'll be able to live quite happily with that knowing that Suzie and Rachel have donated to my Challenge. The shows presenter Nick Hewer despite having more money than you, me, Rachel and Suzie put together unfortunately wasn't as forthcoming. Money to money as the saying goes.

However by the time I have completed the first Challenge we have smashed our second target, consequently we up the ante by doubling it to two thousand pounds. It's reassuring for me given the arduous physical efforts involved to see that each separate Challenge has the desired effect of bringing in several donations not to mention the messages of support and words of encouragement we receive from our supporters which also helps to boost my morale and motivation. Something else we find quite surprising and humbling is the number of supporters who become repeat donors during the course of the Challenge.

I completed my third and final Challenge on the 10th July but we didn't close the fundraiser there and then deciding to officially wrap it up when the Tour de France finished on Sunday 24th with Chris Froome taking his third victory thereby entering the record books in the illustrious company of Greg Lemond, Louison Bobet and Philip Thys (pronounced Tace) the only other three time winners. By doing this we are able to capture the donations of those who were maybe waiting to see if I would actually complete the Challenge and potentially a few stragglers who prompted by the popularity of the Tour and Froomes victory might consider my efforts worthy of a few quid.

By the end of the Challenge we had raised the grand amount of £2,050.00 but have also hopefully managed to raise awareness by highlighting the terrible treatment these magnificent animals are forced to endure. To say we are proud, thankful and satisfied even humbled would be an understatement but there's also a sense of relief and incredulity that the Challenge did so well.

Could we possibly have done better and raised even more money? Well I suppose we could after all hindsight is a wonderful thing and we did learn several lessons during the Challenge. We could have employed other fundraising tactics such as holding coffee mornings or online auctions but these methods are quite time consuming and require a lot of organisation. My wife knows this better than anyone as since our Challenge she has run two very successful online auctions in aid of Podenco rescues both raising in excess of two thousand pounds.

Whilst on the whole the Challenge was a very positive experience there were a few negative incidents which unfortunately came from people actually involved with animal rescue which completely flabbergasted us. Before I removed my rose tinted glasses I imagined that everyone involved in animal rescue would be willing to help each other no matter what for the benefit of the cause but unfortunately this proved not to be the case. What we discovered is that there are a lot of egos involved in animal rescue. As in all walks of life we realise that there are those people who are too arrogant, selfish and precious of what is theirs to share and help the less fortunate.

During the Challenge we ended up in a war of words with the administrators of the American run *Million Paw March for Justice*, supporters of a large rescue in Spain called 112 Carlota Galgos when they took umbrage at us posting on their Facebook page advertising our Challenge. The post was subsequently deleted.

In the process of organising the Challenge I had the bright idea of including Galgos del Sol, a very prominent and successful rescue run by an expat, as a recipient of our fundraiser as I felt it would massively increase the exposure of our Challenge and generate a number of donations. At first they were very interested to be involved until we mentioned the other rescues we were helping at which point they declined stating that they thought it would confuse their supporters if their donations were also going to other rescues. So they were happy to be the sole recipients but not so happy to share. If somebody I didn't know and had no connection with offered me free cash in return for a bit of advertising and networking on social media I'd bite their hand off and I'd also be sure to explain to my supporters where the money was going and why. I'm convinced had they been involved we would have raised an awful lot more money which would have helped everyone especially our chosen recipients who being quite small organisations have a much harder time keeping their heads above water.

Throughout the writing of this book a question kept entering my head which has maybe also crossed your mind, that is 'Are any of the proceeds being donated to charity?' My intention wasn't to write a book for financial gain but to create a diary for myself of events in my life that I'm very proud of. However if this book does ever see the light of day, I doubt it'll be a bestseller nor am I likely to become the next Tim Moore (prolific cycling writer), I believe it my moral obligation to give a percentage of any earnings to my chosen charities.

Call me a socialist but I believe in an egalitarian distribution of wealth.

'When the spirits are low, when the day appears dark, when work becomes monotonous, when hope hardly seems worth having, just mount a bicycle and go out for a spin down the road, without thought on anything but the ride you are taking.'
Sir Arthur Conan Doyle (Novelist)

Here are some of the messages of support left by people who very kindly donated:-

'Thank you for helping the animal charities, I know how hard Jayne and Sally work at ARC and every little counts. We are with you all the way.'

'How wonderful doing something you love whilst raising funds for great causes.'

'Good luck on an amazing challenge. My beautiful greyhound came from KGR so a charity dear to my heart.'

'Well done for embarking on such a challenge for such worthy causes, you are an inspiration.'

Epilogue

'Bicycles may change but Cycling is timeless'
Zapata Espinoza (journalist)

Boxing Day 2016
Fleetwood, Lancashire

My wife and I had been invited by our very good friends Paul and Caroline the proprietors of Twelve Restaurant and Outside Caterers to watch the match at Fleetwood Town football club and enjoy the VIP hospitality that they provide there. It was an intimate gathering of family and a few close friends enjoying a pre match Christmas lunch then back to theirs afterward for a proper knees up.

 Several conversations were taking place around the table when I overheard my wife mention our Challenge from earlier that year. I was seated next to Caroline's brother in law Jamie, whom I had met previously on several occasions, he's an affable sort of chap but does let himself down with his terrible sense of humour and seemingly endless repertoire of terrible jokes. Both he and I listened to Chriss as she regaled the group with tales of the Challenge and generally made me sound like a much better cyclist than I actually am. I consider myself to be a fairly self-effacing and magnanimous kind of person but as a proud wife Chriss is always happy to promote my accomplishments.

 I recall us being sat in a beachside bar in Majorca on a beautifully warm late spring afternoon a few weeks after my first experience of 'the hell of the north' when three MAMILS pulled up, parked their bikes outside and sat at the table next to us. They ordered a bottle of wine as I excused myself and went to the toilet. By the time I'd returned they were sat in awe and admiration as my wife eagerly told them of my exploits on the pave.

 Jamie asked 'How much did you actually raise then?'

 'Two thousand and fifty pounds' was my proud response.

'And how much did it cost you to do the three races?' Jamie enquired.

I considered his question for a few moments doing a quick calculation in my head and figured the amounts were pretty much about the same give or take.

I told him this and his reply caught me somewhat off guard.

'So you could have just donated the money to charity then?'

'Well yes I suppose I could but I had always planned on doing those races anyway, which actually means I wouldn't have had two grand to give to charity' I said.

I continued 'Besides the Challenge wasn't just about money, it was about raising awareness to the awful treatment of Spanish hunting dogs and racing greyhounds as well as encouraging people interested in getting a dog to adopt one that has been rescued rather buying a puppy from a breeder.' trying not to sound too much like a pompous sanctimonious twat.

Jamie nodded then asked 'So what's your next challenge for charity going to be?'

'I don't think there's going to be another' I said.

'Really' said Jamie sounding surprised 'and why's that?'

'Well' I began 'as rewarding and successful as the Challenge was and as proud as I am of what we achieved, at times it was quite stressful and demanding. I never realised that fundraising would be such hard work and that asking people for money so difficult. In the past all the cycling I have done has purely been for my own self-gratification whereas with the events I'd chosen for the Challenge I felt a lot of pressure to not only succeed but also to put in a performance that I deemed worthy of the people who were backing me and the reason for doing them. Also keeping all the social media updated took up a lot of our free time but I wanted the Challenge to have a high profile and raise awareness as much as possible.'

Present day (2017)

I'm still riding my bike, though probably not with the same focus as when I was training for the Challenge, and hope to be for many more years to come. Having said that I have just recently finished another of cycling's monuments Liege-Bastogne-Liege which was an incredibly tough and miserable day out. One hundred hypothermic miles in atrocious weather up hill and down dale in the Ardennes region, whoever said Belgium was flat need not give up their day job to become a travel guide. There are still a few events I'd like to add to my palmares and a few that for logistical reasons will probably never be ticked off. I'd like to complete another 'hell of the north' which would put three cobblestones on my mantelpiece and maybe another Ronde as the route has been altered to again include the iconic cobbled climb of Muur Van Geraardsbergen. Next year I'm committed to participating in the Gent-Wevelgem Cyclo, a Belgian semi classic, as it will be the one hundredth anniversary of the end of the Great War, with the route traversing many of the battlefields of Flanders and actually passing through the Menin Gate which will allow me to pay my respects to relatives and all those other fallen heroes.

In the writing of this work I've tried to not pull any punches and be as honest and as objective as possible. All the events portrayed did actually happen or at least how I remember them happening. Any factual inaccuracies are entirely my fault or of the internet pages I used for research purposes and all opinions are my own, if you don't like them well tough shit I'm afraid. And, in this age of political correctness gone mad if I've said anything that offends you, again tough shit you're free to read something else.

Here's what our chosen charities had to say about the Challenge:–

Jalon Valley ARC
Well done Ritchie, ARC are so proud to have you as our supercyclist. We can't thank you enough for what you have done for us and the other doggie Rescues. We are hoping to make a fenced play area so this will go a long way to help. Once again thank you.

Starfish Dog Rescue
This lovely man who adopted a lovely Galgo from us in the past and gave him such a wonderful home has managed to raise over £2,000 for dog rescues and we were honoured to be one of the 3 Rescues they choose to fundraise for so we have gratefully received

today a donation of £683.33. Its donations like these that keep us going and help so much when we take on the more vulnerable dogs of this world- so thank you Ritchie so much, it's a massive achievement what you did and I hope the other rescues are as grateful as us for this donation. Thank you and thank you for being such a lovely family you and your wife for the lovely home you gave our Mr Spencer. xx

Kent Greyhound Rescue

Ritch Greenwood has successfully finished his 3 Tour Challenge and has raised an incredible £2,050.00, we are sure it was an amazing experience for him but also a really tough physical way to raise money for charity, so we are all in awe of Ritch. I think it is summed up very well in a post on his Facebook page, so well put we agree with it all. Ritch has adopted 2 dogs from Spain, one from us via Jalon Valley ARC and one from Starfish so the money raised has been split equally between the 3 Rescues. We are so grateful for our donation of £683.33, we are all volunteers so all the money donated to KGR does all go to helping the dogs.

The Facebook post that was mentioned was written by an old friend, Nigel Lewin and I wholeheartedly agree that he sums it up perfectly. This is what he said:-

'Well done both of you.

For any Challenge to be valid, I always think there has to be a possibility of failure, and I think you set a Challenge that was worthy because you had to train and dig deep. It wasn't just the efforts of the bike rides though- many people just set up a Just Giving page (or whatever they're called) and leave it at that. You didn't do that; you set up a webpage, you gave information about the Challenge itself and continuous updates to make people feel that they were with you, which I think was important- and now you've finished it off with a public thankyou and…….oh fuck, where's the tissues…..!

Seriously, great effort xx'

It's been emotional.

'Ride as much or as little, as long or as short as you feel. But ride.'
Eddy Merckx (the greatest cyclist of all time)

All the social media information relating to the Challenge can be found at the following links:-

www.greenwoodland.wixsite.com/ritchs3tc
www.facebook.com/Ritchs3tc
www.twitter.com/Ritch_3TC
www.instagram.com/ritch_3tc
www.gofundme.com/Ritch_3TC

Afterword

I am grace and beauty and Greyhound is my name,
I'm elegance personified but speed's my claim to fame
I run and run and run to make money for the Man
but I'm often tossed aside when I no longer can.
But I'm one of the lucky ones, I've managed to survive
so many of my fellow Greys are no longer alive.
Thrown away like garbage, abandoned and abused,
no longer making money, their usefulness all used!
But look into my eyes and you will see into my heart,
Have thoughts and feelings too, I suffer for my art!
Look into my heart again you'll see my needs are few,
A walk, some food, a comfy bed, to spend some time with you
So look into your own heart and tell me that you care,
Look into your own heart and tell me I am there!

Poem written by Mandy McBride

Acknowledgements

Without doubt the most influential person during the Challenge has been my amazing wife Chriss, without her it's very likely that the Challenge would never have got off the ground or been quite as successful as it turned out to be.

She spent many hours of her limited free time putting together all the social media stuff, creating Facebook, Twitter and Instagram accounts as well as designing and building our very own website which quite frankly I wouldn't have had a clue how to do!

She was also instrumental in the updating of these pages and networking to increase the exposure of the Challenge, receiving a good luck tweet from Countdowns lexicographer Suzie Dent on the day of L'Etape was all her doing.

She was also responsible for initially contacting our chosen charities, getting them on board and their continuous involvement with the Challenge as well as handling all the fundraising monies and finally distributing the donations.

Although Chriss didn't do any cycling I know that she was with me every pedal turn of the way.

If my wife Chriss has been the most influential then the most important people were those who donated their hard earned cash and supported my Challenge. Without them the Challenge wouldn't have been as nearly as successful as it turned out to be. All donations no matter the amount were so humbly and gratefully received but I do feel the need to mention a few individuals for their incredible generosity, they are in no particular order Nicola Harrison, Eileen Aspinall and Nigel Lewin.

The people deserving of my gratitude for rescuing Olive are Jayne Webb, Sally Mason and everyone associated with Jalon Valley A.R.C., the good people of Kent Greyhound Rescue for being involved with the transport of Olive to the UK and finding her a foster mum, the wonderful Laura Cording who took such good care of her before she finally came to us.

Spencer was rescued by the lovely Gill Minnican along with Sue Jones, Sherlie Bradley and all those involved with Starfish Dog Rescue and its affiliate Little Starfish based in Mazarron, Spain. A notable mention has to be made of the very special lady who fostered Spencer when he came to the UK, Miss Julie Wright who did so much voluntary work for Starfish. Sadly Julie passed away very suddenly in the autumn of 2016 and the world of animal rescue will be so much the worse off because of her loss.

God bless Julie, you will be sorely missed.

It would be extremely remiss of me not to acknowledge all the various Charities and Organisations both here in the United Kingdom and overseas involved in animal rescue and welfare who do such amazing work often facing terrible circumstances and frequently on such tight budgets that in many cases they end up funding projects using their own personal incomes.

You are all Angels.